Kaplan Publishing are constantly finding new ways to make a difference to your studies and our exciting online resources really do offer something different to students looking for exam success.

This book comes with free MyKaplan online resources so that you can study anytime, anywhere. **This free online resource is not sold separately and is included in the price of the book.**

Having purchased this book, you have access to the following online study materials:

| CONTENT | AAT | |
| --- | --- | --- |
| | Text | Kit |
| iPaper version of the book | ✓ | ✓ |
| Progress tests with instant answers | ✓ | |
| Mock assessments online | ✓ | ✓ |
| Material updates | ✓ | ✓ |

D0543290

### How to access your online resources

Kaplan Financial students will already have a MyKaplan account and these extra resources will be available to you online. You do not need to register again, as this process was completed when you enrolled. If you are having problems accessing online materials, please ask your course administrator.

If you are already a registered MyKaplan user go to www.MyKaplan.co.uk and log in. Select the 'add a book' feature and enter the ISBN number of this book and the unique pass key at the bottom of this card. Then click 'finished' or 'add another book'. You may add as many books as you have purchased from this screen.

If you purchased through Kaplan Flexible Learning or via the Kaplan Publishing website you will automatically receive an e-mail invitation to MyKaplan. Please register your details using this email to gain access to your content. If you do not receive the e-mail or book content, please contact Kaplan Flexible Learning.

If you are a new user register at www.MyKaplan.co.uk and click on the link contained in the email we sent you to activate your account. Then select the 'add a book' feature, enter the ISBN number of this book and the unique pass key at the bottom of this card. Then click 'finished' or 'add another book'.

## Your Code and Information

This code can only be used once for the registration of one book online. This registration and your online content will expire when the final sittings for the examinations covered by this book have taken place. Please allow one hour from the time you submit your book details for us to process your request.

---

Please scratch the film to access your MyKaplan code.

Please be aware that this code is case-sensitive and you will need to include the dashes within the passcode, but not when entering the ISBN. For further technical support, please visit www.MyKaplan.co.uk

# AAT

# AQ2016

---

# Bookkeeping Transactions

---

# EXAM KIT

This Exam Kit supports study for the following AAT qualifications:

AAT Foundation Certificate in Accounting – Level 2

AAT Foundation Diploma in Accounting and Business – Level 2

AAT Foundation Certificate in Bookkeeping – Level 2

AAT Foundation Award in Accounting Software – Level 2

AAT Level 2 Award in Accounting Skills to Run Your Business

AAT Foundation Certificate in Accounting at SCQF Level 5

**British Library Cataloguing-in-Publication Data**

A catalogue record for this book is available from the British Library.

Published by:

Kaplan Publishing UK

Unit 2 The Business Centre

Molly Millar's Lane

Wokingham

Berkshire

RG41 2QZ

ISBN: 978-1-78415-584-1

© Kaplan Financial Limited, 2016

Printed and bound in Great Britain.

# CONTENTS

---

**Features in this exam kit**

In addition to providing a wide ranging bank of real exam style questions, we have also included in this kit:

- unit-specific information and advice on exam technique

- our recommended approach to make your revision for this particular unit as effective as possible.

---

You will find a wealth of other resources to help you with your studies on the AAT website:

www.aat.org.uk/

Quality and accuracy are of the utmost importance to us so if you spot an error in any of our products, please send an email to mykaplanreporting@kaplan.com with full details, or follow the link to the feedback form in MyKaplan.

Our Quality Co-ordinator will work with our technical team to verify the error and take action to ensure it is corrected in future editions.

# UNIT-SPECIFIC INFORMATION

## THE EXAM

### FORMAT OF THE ASSESSMENT

The assessment will comprise ten independent tasks. Students will be assessed by computer-based assessment.

In any one assessment, students may not be assessed on all content, or on the full depth or breadth of a piece of content. The content assessed may change over time to ensure validity of assessment, but all assessment criteria will be tested over time.

The learning outcomes for this unit are as follows:

| | Learning outcome | Weighting |
|---|---|---|
| 1 | Understand financial transactions within a bookkeeping system | 10% |
| 2 | Process customer transactions | 10% |
| 3 | Process supplier transactions | 15% |
| 4 | Process receipts and payments | 25% |
| 5 | Process transactions through the ledgers to the trial balance | 40% |
| | Total | 100% |

**Time allowed**

2 hours

### PASS MARK

The pass mark for all AAT CBAs is 70%.

🕐 **Always keep your eye on the clock and make sure you attempt all questions!**

## DETAILED SYLLABUS

The detailed syllabus and study guide written by the AAT can be found at:

www.aat.org.uk/

# INDEX TO QUESTIONS AND ANSWERS

# EXAM TECHNIQUE

- **Do not skip any of the material** in the syllabus.

- **Read each question** *very* carefully.

- **Double-check your answer** before committing yourself to it.

- Answer **every** question – if you do not know an answer to a multiple choice question or true/false question, you don't lose anything by guessing. Think carefully before you **guess**.

- If you are answering a multiple-choice question, **eliminate first those answers that you know are wrong.** Then choose the most appropriate answer from those that are left.

- **Don't panic** if you realise you've answered a question incorrectly. Getting one question wrong will not mean the difference between passing and failing.

## Computer-based exams – tips

- Do not attempt a CBA until you have **completed all study material** relating to it.

- On the AAT website there is a CBA demonstration. It is **ESSENTIAL** that you attempt this before your real CBA. You will become familiar with how to move around the CBA screens and the way that questions are formatted, increasing your confidence and speed in the actual exam.

- Be sure you understand how to use the **software** before you start the exam. If in doubt, ask the assessment centre staff to explain it to you.

- Questions are **displayed on the screen** and answers are entered using keyboard and mouse. At the end of the exam, you are given a certificate showing the result you have achieved.

- In addition to the traditional multiple-choice question type, CBAs will also contain **other types of questions**, such as number entry questions, drag and drop, true/false, pick lists or drop down menus or hybrids of these.

- In some CBAs you will have to type in complete computations or written answers.

- You need to be sure you **know how to answer questions** of this type before you sit the exam, through practice.

KAPLAN PUBLISHING

# KAPLAN'S RECOMMENDED REVISION APPROACH

## QUESTION PRACTICE IS THE KEY TO SUCCESS

Success in professional examinations relies upon you acquiring a firm grasp of the required knowledge at the tuition phase. In order to be able to do the questions, knowledge is essential.

However, the difference between success and failure often hinges on your exam technique on the day and making the most of the revision phase of your studies.

The **Kaplan Study Text** is the starting point, designed to provide the underpinning knowledge to tackle all questions. However, in the revision phase, poring over text books is not the answer.

**Kaplan Pocket Notes** are designed to help you quickly revise a topic area; however you then need to practise questions. There is a need to progress to exam style questions as soon as possible, and to tie your exam technique and technical knowledge together.

**The importance of question practice cannot be over-emphasised.**

The recommended approach below is designed by expert tutors in the field, in conjunction with their knowledge of the examiner and the specimen assessment.

**You need to practise as many questions as possible in the time you have left.**

## OUR AIM

Our aim is to get you to the stage where you can attempt exam questions confidently, to time, in a closed book environment, with no supplementary help (i.e. to simulate the real examination experience).

Practising your exam technique is also vitally important for you to assess your progress and identify areas of weakness that may need more attention in the final run up to the examination.

In order to achieve this we recognise that initially you may feel the need to practice some questions with open book help.

**Good exam technique is vital.**

# THE KAPLAN REVISION PLAN

## Stage 1: Assess areas of strengths and weaknesses

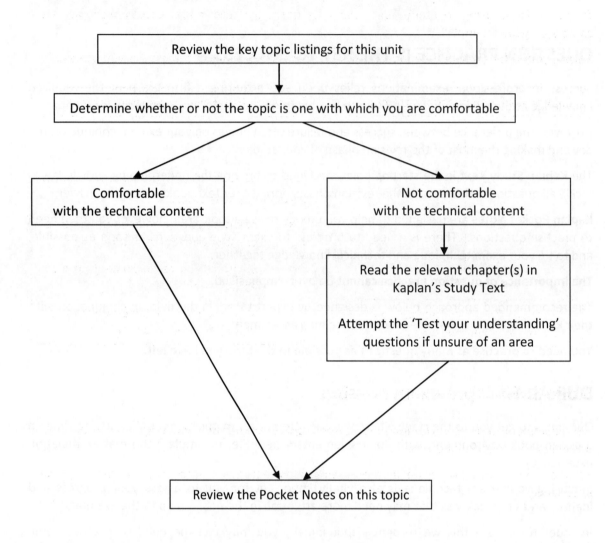

## Stage 2: Practice questions

Follow the order of revision of topics as presented in this Kit and attempt the questions in the order suggested.

Try to avoid referring to Study Texts and your notes and the model answer until you have completed your attempt.

Review your attempt with the model answer and assess how much of the answer you achieved.

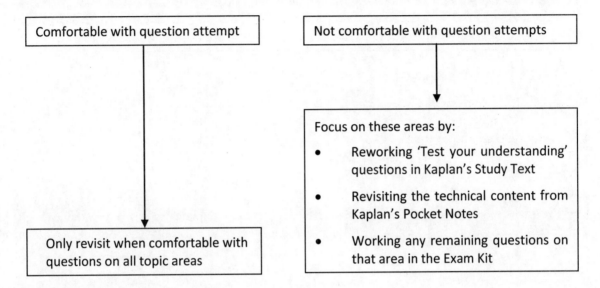

| Comfortable with question attempt | Not comfortable with question attempts |

Only revisit when comfortable with questions on all topic areas

Focus on these areas by:

- Reworking 'Test your understanding' questions in Kaplan's Study Text

- Revisiting the technical content from Kaplan's Pocket Notes

- Working any remaining questions on that area in the Exam Kit

## Stage 3: Final pre-exam revision

We recommend that you **attempt at least one mock examination** containing a set of previously unseen exam-standard questions.

Attempt the mock CBA online in timed, closed book conditions to simulate the real exam experience.

# Section 1

# PRACTICE QUESTIONS

## MAKING ENTRIES IN DAY BOOKS

**1    SDB**

Sales invoices have been prepared and partially entered in the sales day-book, as shown below.

(a)    **Complete the entries in the sales day-book by inserting the appropriate figures for each invoice.**

(b)    **Total the last five columns of the sales day-book.**

**Sales day-book**

| Date 20XX | Details | Invoice number | Total £ | VAT £ | Net £ | Sales type 1 £ | Sales type 2 £ |
|---|---|---|---|---|---|---|---|
| 31 Dec | Poonams | 105 | 3,600 | | | | 3,000 |
| 31 Dec | D. Taylor | 106 | | 1,280 | | 6,400 | |
| 31 Dec | Smiths | 107 | 3,840 | | 3,200 | | 3,200 |
| | **Totals** | | | | | | |

**2    FREDDIE LTD**

Purchase invoices have been received and partially entered in the purchases day-book of Freddie Ltd, as shown below.

(a)    **Complete the first two entries in the purchases day-book by inserting the appropriate figures for each invoice.**

(b)    **Complete the final entry in the purchases day book by inserting the appropriate figures from the following invoice.**

---

**Novot & Co**

**5 Pheasant Way, Essex, ES9 8BN**

**VAT Registration No. 453 098 541**

**Invoice No. 2176**

Freddie Ltd

9 Banbury Street

Sheffield

31 July 20XX

| | |
|---|---:|
| 10 boxes of product code 14212 @ £400 each | £4,000 |
| VAT | £800 |
| Total | £4,800 |
| Payment terms 30 days | |

**Purchases day-book**

| Date 20XX | Details | Invoice number | Total £ | VAT £ | Net £ | Product 14211 £ | Product 14212 £ |
|---|---|---|---|---|---|---|---|
| 31 July | Box Ltd | 2177 | | | 800 | 800 | |
| 31 July | Shrew Ltd | 2175 | | 2,400 | | 12,000 | |
| 31 July | Novot & Co | 2176 | | | | | |
| | **Totals** | | | | | | |

**3      MAHINDRA LTD**

Sales invoices have been received and partially entered in the sales day-book of Mahindra Ltd, as shown below.

(a)      **Complete the entries in the sales day-book by inserting the appropriate figures for each invoice.**

(b)      **Total the last five columns of the sales day-book.**

**Sales day-book**

| Date 20XX | Details | Invoice number | Total £ | VAT £ | Net £ | Sales type 1 £ | Sales type 2 £ |
|---|---|---|---|---|---|---|---|
| 31 Jan | Square Ltd | 3567 | | | 1,000 | 1,000 | |
| 31 Jan | Oval & Co | 3568 | | 1,600 | | | 8,000 |
| 31 Jan | Diamond Ltd | 3569 | 13,200 | | | | 11,000 |
| 31 Jan | Triangle Ltd | 3570 | | 1,320 | | 6,600 | |
| | Totals | | | | | | |

# CODING

**4      LEO LTD**

Leo Ltd codes all sales invoices with a customer code AND a general ledger code. A selection of the codes used is given below.

| Customer | Customer account code |
|---|---|
| DEF Ltd | DEF14 |
| Gamma Production | GAM27 |
| MBG Co | MBG20 |
| Harley Interiors | HAR18 |
| Clarkson Wholesale | CLA16 |

| Item | General ledger code |
|---|---|
| Standard bath | GL529 |
| Standard washbasin | GL526 |
| Luxury taps | GL530 |
| Bathroom cabinet | GL521 |
| Toilet | GL535 |
| Standard light switch | GL528 |

This is an invoice sent to a customer.

| **Leo Ltd** |
|---|
| **121 Apple Lane** |
| **Cuddington, CU9 8EF** |
| **VAT Registration No. 398 2774 01** |

| DEF Ltd | |
|---|---|
| 51 Neville Street, | |
| Manchester, M1 4PJ | 18 Aug 20XX |
| 10 ........ Luxury taps for washbasin @ £8.80 each | £88.00 |
| VAT | £17.60 |
| Total | £105.60 |

(a)    **Select which codes would be used to code this invoice.**

| General ledger code | Picklist: DEF14, GL529, GAM27, GL 526, GL530, GL521, GL535, CLA16 |
|---|---|
| Customer account code | Picklist: GL530, GL526, DEF14, MBG20, HAR18, GL521, GL528, GAM27 |

(b)    **Why is it useful to use a customer code?**

|  |
|---|
|  |

Picklist: To help when inventory (stock) taking

To help when completing a tax return

To help find the total amount due to a supplier

To help trace orders and amounts due from particular customers

**5     ELLA'S PAINTS**

Ella's Paint's codes all purchases invoices with a supplier code AND a general ledger code. A selection of the codes used is given below.

| Supplier | Supplier account code |
|---|---|
| Peak Ltd | PEA27 |
| Marker Production | MAR19 |
| MEG & Co | MEG20 |
| Farley Interiors | FAR12 |
| Hammond Wholesale | HAM16 |

| Item | General ledger code |
|---|---|
| White Paint | GL360 |
| Standard Roller | GL395 |
| Standard Brush | GL320 |
| Yellow Paint | GL370 |
| Roller tray | GL330 |

This is an invoice received from a supplier.

| **Meg & Co** | |
|---|---|
| **12 Barker Street** | |
| **Leeds L1 4NZ** | |
| **VAT Registration No. 402 2958 02** | |
| Ella's Paints | |
| 19 Edmund St, | 18 Feb 20XX |
| Newcastle, NE6 5DJ | |
| | |
| 20  ........ standard rollers @ £2.30 each | £46.00 |
| VAT | £9.20 |
| Total | £55.20 |

(a)     **Select which codes would be used to code this invoice.**

| General ledger code | Picklist: PEA27, MAR19, GL360, MEG20, GL395, FAR12, GL330, HAM 16 |
|---|---|
| Supplier account code | Picklist: PEA27, MAR19, GL360, MEG20, GL395, FAR12, GL330, HAM 16 |

(b)     **Why is it useful to use a supplier code?**

Picklist: To help when inventory (stock) taking

To help when completing a tax return

To help trace orders and amounts due to particular suppliers

To help trace orders and amounts due from particular customers

## 6     ROBERTO & CO

Roberto & Co codes all purchase invoices with a supplier code AND a general ledger code. A selection of the codes used is given below.

| Supplier | Supplier account code |
|----------|----------------------|
| Alex Ltd | ALE1 |
| Toyworld | TOY10 |
| Pudding and Co | PUD4 |
| Springclean Ltd | SPR7 |
| Spoonaway | SPO3 |

| Item | General ledger code |
|------|--------------------|
| Food | GL18 |
| Toys | GL72 |
| Stationery | GL45 |
| Cleaning Equipment | GL78 |
| Kitchenware | GL29 |

This is an invoice received from a supplier.

| Alex Ltd |
|---|
| **CherryWay, Haworth, BD22 9HQ** |
| **VAT Registration No. 248 2764 00** |

| | |
|---|---|
| Roberto & Co | |
| Roberto House | |
| Ashton, AS2 8TN | 1 Jan 20XX |
| | |
| 10 ........ teddy bears @ £4 each | £40.00 |
| | |
| VAT | £ 8.00 |
| | |
| Total | £48.00 |

(a)   **Select which codes would be used to code this invoice.**

| Supplier account code | Picklist: ALE1, TOY10, PUD4, SPR7, SPO3, GL18, GL72, GL45, GL78, GL29 |
|---|---|
| General ledger code | Picklist: ALE1, TOY10, PUD4, SPR7, SPO3, GL18, GL72, GL45, GL78, GL29 |

(b)   **Why is it necessary to use a general ledger code?**

|  |
|---|
|  |

Picklist: To help when filling in a VAT return

To help when bar coding an item of inventory

To help find the total amount owing to a supplier

To help calculate expense incurred in a GL account

# TRANSFERRING DATA FROM DAY BOOKS TO LEDGERS

**7 LADY LTD**

Given below is the purchases day book for Lady Ltd

| Date | Invoice No. | Code | Supplier | Total | VAT | Net |
|------|-------------|------|----------|-------|-----|-----|
| 1 Dec | 03582 | PL210 | M Brown | 300.00 | 50.00 | 250.00 |
| 5 Dec | 03617 | PL219 | H Madden | 183.55 | 30.59 | 152.96 |
| 7 Dec | 03622 | PL227 | L Singh | 132.60 | 22.10 | 110.50 |
| 10 Dec | 03623 | PL228 | A Stevens | 90.00 | 15.00 | 75.00 |
| 18 Dec | 03712 | PL301 | N Shema | 197.08 | 32.84 | 164.24 |
| | | | **Totals** | **903.23** | **150.53** | **752.70** |

**You are required to:**

- Post the totals of the purchases day book to the general ledger accounts given

- Post the invoices to the payables' accounts in the subsidiary ledger given.

**General ledger**

### Purchases ledger control account

| | £ | | £ |
|---|---|---|---|
| | | 1 Dec Balance b/d | 5,103.90 |

### VAT account

| | £ | | £ |
|---|---|---|---|
| | | 1 Dec Balance b/d | 526.90 |

### Purchases account

| | £ | | £ |
|---|---|---|---|
| 1 Dec balance b/d | 22,379.52 | | |

**Subsidiary ledger**

### M Brown

| | £ | | £ |
|---|---|---|---|
| | | 1 Dec Balance b/d | 68.50 |

### H Madden

| | £ | | | £ |
|---|---|---|---|---|
| | | 1 Dec Balance b/d | | 286.97 |

### L Singh

| | £ | | | £ |
|---|---|---|---|---|
| | | 1 Dec Balance b/d | | 125.89 |

### A Stevens

| | £ | | | £ |
|---|---|---|---|---|
| | | 1 Dec Balance b/d | | 12.36 |

### N Shema

| | £ | | | £ |
|---|---|---|---|---|
| | | 1 Dec Balance b/d | | 168.70 |

## 8    BUTTONS LTD

The following transactions all took place on 31 July and have been entered into the purchases day book of Buttons Ltd as shown below. No entries have yet been made into the ledger system.

| Date 20XX | Details | Invoice number | Total £ | VAT £ | Net £ |
|---|---|---|---|---|---|
| 31 July | Peak & Co | 1720 | 6,240 | 1,040 | 5,200 |
| 31 July | Max Ltd | 1721 | 12,720 | 2,120 | 10,600 |
| 31 July | McIntyre Wholesale | 1722 | 5,760 | 960 | 4,800 |
| 31 July | Pigmy Ltd | 1723 | 3,744 | 624 | 3,120 |
| | **Totals** | | 28,464 | 4,744 | 23,720 |

(a)    **What will be the entries in the purchases ledger?**

| Account name | Amount £ | Debit ✓ | Credit ✓ |
|---|---|---|---|
| | | | |
| | | | |
| | | | |
| | | | |

Picklist: Peak & Co, Purchases, Sales ledger control, Purchases returns, McIntyre Wholesale, Sales, Purchases ledger control, Max Ltd, Sales returns, VAT, Pigmy Ltd

(b)    **What will be the entries in the general ledger?**

| Account name | Amount £ | Debit ✓ | Credit ✓ |
|---|---|---|---|
|  |  |  |  |
|  |  |  |  |
|  |  |  |  |

Picklist: Purchases ledger control, Sales, Sales ledger control, Purchases, VAT

## 9    SPARKY LTD

The following credit transactions all took place on 31 July and have been entered into the sales returns day-book of Sparky Ltd as shown below. No entries have yet been made in the ledgers.

**Sales returns day-book**

| Date 20XX | Details | Credit note number | Total £ | VAT £ | Net £ |
|---|---|---|---|---|---|
| 31 July | Clarkson Ltd | 150C | 1,680 | 280 | 1,400 |
| 31 July | Kyle & Co | 151C | 720 | 120 | 600 |
|  | Totals |  | 2,400 | 400 | 2,000 |

(a)    **What will be the entries in the sales ledger?**

**Sales ledger**

| Account name | Amount £ | Debit ✓ | Credit ✓ |
|---|---|---|---|
|  |  |  |  |
|  |  |  |  |

Picklist: Net, Purchases, Purchases ledger control, Clarkson Ltd, Purchases returns, Sales, Sales ledger control, Sales returns, Kyle & Co, Total, VAT

(b)    **What will be the entries in the general ledger?**

**General ledger**

| Account name | Amount £ | Debit ✓ | Credit ✓ |
|---|---|---|---|
|  |  |  |  |
|  |  |  |  |
|  |  |  |  |

Picklist: Kyle & Co, Net, Purchases, Purchases ledger control, Purchases returns, Sales, Sales ledger control, Sales returns, Clarkson Ltd, Total, VAT

## 10 LOUIS LTD

The following transactions all took place on 31 Jan and have been entered into the sales day book of Louis Ltd as shown below. No entries have yet been made into the ledger system.

| Date 20XX | Details | Invoice number | Total £ | VAT £ | Net £ |
|---|---|---|---|---|---|
| 31 Jan | Sheep & Co | 1400 | 3,840 | 640 | 3,200 |
| 31 Jan | Cow Ltd | 1401 | 11,760 | 1,960 | 9,800 |
| 31 Jan | Chicken & Partners | 1402 | 6,720 | 1,120 | 5,600 |
| 31 Jan | Pig Ltd | 1403 | 14,496 | 2,416 | 12,080 |
| | **Totals** | | 36,816 | 6,136 | 30,680 |

(a) **What will be the entries in the sales ledger?**

| Account name | Amount £ | Debit ✓ | Credit ✓ |
|---|---|---|---|
| | | | |
| | | | |
| | | | |
| | | | |

Picklist: Sheep & Co, Purchases, Sales ledger control, Cow Ltd, Purchases returns, Sales, Chicken & Partners, Purchases ledger control, Sales returns, VAT, Pig Ltd

(b) **What will be the entries in the general ledger?**

| Account name | Amount £ | Debit ✓ | Credit ✓ |
|---|---|---|---|
| | | | |
| | | | |
| | | | |

Picklist: Purchases ledger control, Sales, Sales ledger control, Purchases, VAT

## 11 THOMAS & TILLY

The following credit transactions all took place on 31 Jan and have been entered into the purchase returns day-book of Thomas & Tilly as shown below. No entries have yet been made in the ledgers.

**Purchase returns day-book**

| Date 20XX | Details | Credit note number | Total £ | VAT £ | Net £ |
|---|---|---|---|---|---|
| 31 Jan | May Ltd | 230C | 1,920 | 320 | 1,600 |
| 31 Jan | Hammond & Co | 231C | 1,200 | 200 | 1,000 |
| | **Totals** | | 3,120 | 520 | 2,600 |

(a)   **What will be the entries in the purchases ledger?**

**Purchase ledger**

| Account name | Amount £ | Debit ✓ | Credit ✓ |
|---|---|---|---|
| | | | |
| | | | |

Picklist: Net, Purchases, Purchases ledger control, May Ltd, Purchases returns, Sales, Sales ledger control, Sales returns, VAT, Hammond & Co, Total.

(b)   **What will be the entries in the general ledger?**

**General ledger**

| Account name | Amount £ | Debit ✓ | Credit ✓ |
|---|---|---|---|
| | | | |
| | | | |
| | | | |

Picklist: May Ltd, Net, Purchases, Purchases ledger control, Purchases returns, Sales, Sales ledger control, Sales returns, Hammond & Co, Total, VAT

## 12 FINCH'S

The following transactions all took place on 31 Dec and have been entered into the sales day book of Finch's as shown below. No entries have yet been made into the ledger system.

| Date 20XX | Details | Invoice number | Total £ | VAT £ | Net £ |
|---|---|---|---|---|---|
| 31 Dec | Lou and Phil's | 700 | 5,040 | 840 | 4,200 |
| 31 Dec | Eddie and Co | 701 | 10,560 | 1,760 | 8,800 |
| 31 Dec | Noah's Arc | 702 | 2,880 | 480 | 2,400 |
| 31 Dec | Alex and Freddie | 703 | 720 | 120 | 600 |
| | **Totals** | | **19,200** | **3,200** | **16,000** |

(a) **What will be the entries in the sales ledger?**

| Account name | Amount £ | Debit ✓ | Credit ✓ |
|---|---|---|---|
| | | | |
| | | | |
| | | | |
| | | | |

Picklist: Lou and Phil's, Eddie and Co, Noah's Arc, Alex and Freddie, Purchases, Purchases ledger control, Purchases returns, Sales, Sales ledger control, Sales returns, VAT

(b) **What will be the entries in the general ledger?**

| Account name | Amount £ | Debit ✓ | Credit ✓ |
|---|---|---|---|
| | | | |
| | | | |
| | | | |

Picklist: Purchases ledger control, Sales, Sales ledger control, Sales returns, VAT

## 13    JESSICA & CO

The following credit transactions all took place on 31 Dec and have been entered into the purchases returns day-book as shown below. No entries have yet been made in the ledgers.

**Purchases returns day-book**

| Date 20XX | Details | Credit note number | Total £ | VAT £ | Net £ |
|---|---|---|---|---|---|
| 31 Dec | Iona Ltd | 4763 | 1,680 | 280 | 1,400 |
| 31 Dec | Matilda Ltd | 2164 | 4,320 | 720 | 3,600 |
| | Totals | | 6,000 | 1,000 | 5,000 |

(a)    **What will be the entries in the purchases ledger?**

**Purchases ledger**

| Account name | Amount £ | Debit ✓ | Credit ✓ |
|---|---|---|---|
| | | | |
| | | | |

Picklist: Iona Ltd, Matilda Ltd, Net, Purchases, Purchases ledger control, Purchases returns, Sales, Sales ledger control, Sales returns, Total, VAT

(b)    **What will be the entries in the general ledger?**

**General ledger**

| Account name | Amount £ | Debit ✓ | Credit ✓ |
|---|---|---|---|
| | | | |
| | | | |
| | | | |

Picklist: Iona Ltd, Matilda Ltd, Net, Purchases, Purchases ledger control, Purchases returns, Sales, Sales ledger control, Sales returns, VAT, Total

## 14 HORSEY REACH

The following transactions all took place on 31 July and have been entered into the discounts allowed day book of Horsey Reach as shown below. No entries have yet been made into the ledger system.

| Date 20XX | Details | Credit note number | Total £ | VAT £ | Net £ |
|---|---|---|---|---|---|
| 31 July | Ashleigh Buildings | 145 | 36.00 | 6.00 | 30.00 |
| 31 July | 143 WGT | 146 | 54.00 | 9.00 | 45.00 |
| 31 July | McDuff McGregor | 147 | 43.20 | 7.20 | 36.00 |
| 31 July | Cameron Travel | 148 | 93.60 | 15.60 | 78.00 |
| | **Totals** | | 226.80 | 37.80 | 189.00 |

(a) **What will be the entries in the general ledger?**

| Account name | Amount £ | Debit ✓ | Credit ✓ |
|---|---|---|---|
| | | | |
| | | | |
| | | | |

Picklist: 13 WGT, Ashleigh Buildings, Cameron Travel, Discounts Allowed, Discounts Received, McDuff McGregor, Purchases, Purchases ledger control, Sales, Sales ledger control, VAT

(b) **What will be the entries in the subsidiary ledger?**

| Account name | Amount £ | Debit ✓ | Credit ✓ |
|---|---|---|---|
| | | | |
| | | | |
| | | | |
| | | | |

Picklist: 143 WGT, Ashleigh Buildings, Cameron Travel, Discounts Allowed, Discounts Received,  McDuff McGregor, Purchases, Purchases ledger control, Sales, Sales ledger control, VAT

**15    BUTTERFLY BEES**

These are the totals from the discounts received book of Butterfly Bees at the end of the month.

| Total £ | VAT £ | Net £ |
|---|---|---|
| 427.20 | 71.20 | 356.00 |

(a)    **What will be the entries in the general ledger?**

| Account name | Amount £ | Debit ✓ | Credit ✓ |
|---|---|---|---|
|  |  |  |  |
|  |  |  |  |
|  |  |  |  |

One of the entries in the discounts received day book is for a credit note received from Bella Bumps for £20 plus VAT.

(b)    **What will be the entry in the purchases ledger?**

| Account name | Amount £ | Debit ✓ | Credit ✓ |
|---|---|---|---|
|  |  |  |  |

**16    OLIVIA ROSE BRIDAL SUPPLIES**

These are the totals from the discounts allowed book of Olivia Rose Bridal Supplies at the end of the month.

| Total £ | VAT £ | Net £ |
|---|---|---|
| 226.80 | 37.80 | 189.00 |

(a)    **What will be the entries in the general ledger?**

| Account name | Amount £ | Debit ✓ | Credit ✓ |
|---|---|---|---|
|  |  |  |  |
|  |  |  |  |
|  |  |  |  |

One of the entries in the discounts allowed day book is for a credit note sent to Bridezilla for £45 plus VAT.

(b)    **What will be the entry in the sales ledger?**

| Account name | Amount £ | Debit ✓ | Credit ✓ |
|---|---|---|---|
|  |  |  |  |

# THE CASH BOOK

**17    ABC LTD**

There are five payments to be entered in ABC Ltd's cash-book.

**Receipts**

| Received cash with thanks for goods bought.<br>From ABC Ltd, a customer without a credit account.<br><br>Net          £180<br>VAT            £36<br>Total         £216<br><br>*S. Lampard* | Received cash with thanks for goods bought.<br>From ABC Ltd, a customer without a credit account.<br><br>Net          £220<br>VAT            £44<br>Total         £264<br><br>*S Bobbins* | Received cash with thanks for goods bought.<br>ABC Ltd, a customer without a credit account.<br><br>Net          £530<br>(No VAT)<br><br><br>*Penny Rhodes* |

**Cheque book counterfoils**

| Henley's Ltd<br>(Purchase ledger account HEN002)<br><br><br>£4,925<br><br><br><br>000372 | Epic Equipment Maintenance<br>(We have no credit account with this supplier)<br><br>£480 incl VAT<br><br><br><br>000373 |

(a)    **Enter the details from the three receipts and two cheque book stubs into the credit side of the cash-book shown below and total each column.**

**Cash-book – credit side**

| Details | Cash | Bank | VAT | Payables | Cash purchases | Repairs and renewals |
|---|---|---|---|---|---|---|
| Balance b/f | | | | | | |
| S. Lampard | | | | | | |
| S. Bobbins | | | | | | |
| Penny Rhodes | | | | | | |
| Henley's Ltd | | | | | | |
| Epic Equipment Maintenance | | | | | | |
| Total | | | | | | |

There are two cheques from credit customers to be entered in ABC Ltd's cash book:

D. Davies          £851

E. Denholm          £450

(b)    Enter the above details into the debit side of the cash-book and total each column.

**Cash book – debit side**

| Details | Cash | Bank | Receivables |
|---|---|---|---|
| Balance b/f | 1,550 | 7,425 | |
| D Davies | | | |
| E Denholm | | | |
| Total | | | |

(c)    Using your answers to (a) and (b) above calculate the cash balance.

£

(d)    Using your answers to (a) and (b) above calculate the bank balance.

£

(e)    Will the bank balance calculated in (d) above be a debit or credit balance?

Debit/Credit

## 18    BEDS

There are five payments to be entered in Beds' cash-book.

**Receipts**

| Received cash with thanks for goods bought.<br>From Beds, a customer without a credit account.<br><br>Net      £590<br>VAT      £118<br>Total      £708<br><br>A. Blighty Ltd | Received cash with thanks for goods bought.<br>From Beds, a customer without a credit account.<br><br>Net      £190<br>VAT      £38<br>Total      £228<br><br>R Bromby | Received cash with thanks for goods bought.<br>From Beds, a customer without a credit account.<br><br>Net      £230<br>(No VAT)<br><br><br>Roxy Bland |
|---|---|---|

**Cheque book counterfoils**

| Burgess Ltd<br>(Purchase ledger account BUR003)<br><br><br>£2,400<br><br><br><br>000101 | Fast Equipment Repairs<br>(We have no credit account with this supplier)<br><br><br>£96 including VAT<br><br><br><br>000102 |
|---|---|

(a) **Enter the details from the three receipts and two cheque book stubs into the credit side of the cash-book shown below and total each column.**

Cash-book – credit side

| Details | Cash | Bank | VAT | Payables | Cash purchases | Repairs and renewals |
|---------|------|------|-----|----------|----------------|----------------------|
| Balance b/f | | | | | | |
| A. Blighty Ltd | | | | | | |
| R Bromby | | | | | | |
| Roxy Bland | | | | | | |
| Burgess Ltd | | | | | | |
| Fast Equipment Repairs | | | | | | |
| Total | | | | | | |

There are two cheques from credit customers to be entered in Beds' cash book:

A. Barnett          £698

H. Connelly          £250

(b) **Enter the above details into the debit side of the cash-book and total each column.**

Cash book – debit side

| Details | Cash | Bank | Receivables |
|---------|------|------|-------------|
| Balance b/f | 1,175 | 3,825 | |
| A Barnett | | | |
| H Connelly | | | |
| Total | | | |

(c) **Using your answers to (a) and (b) above calculate the cash balance.**

£ 

(d) **Using your answers to (a) and (b) above calculate the bank balance.**

£ 

(e) **Will the bank balance calculated in (d) above be a debit or credit balance?**

Debit/Credit

**19   JO'S**

There are five payments to be entered into Jo's cash-book.

**Receipts**

| | | |
|---|---|---|
| Received cash with thanks for good bought. | Received cash with thanks for good bought. | Received cash with thanks for good bought. |
| From Jo's, a customer without a credit account. | From Jo's, a customer without a credit account. | From Jo's, a customer without a credit account. |
| Net £40 | Net £80 | Net £455 |
| VAT £8 | VAT £16 | (no VAT) |
| Total £48 | Total £96 | |
| T. Hunkin Ltd | Victoria Green | B. Head Ltd |

**Cheque book counterfoils**

| | |
|---|---|
| Smiths Ltd (Purchase ledger account SMI527) | Arrow Valley Stationers (We have no credit account with this supplier) |
| £4,250 | £120 (including VAT) |
| 001456 | 001457 |

(a)   **Enter the details from the three receipts and two cheque book stubs into the credit side of the cash-book shown below and total each column.**

Cash-book – credit side

| Details | Cash | Bank | VAT | Payables | Cash purchases | Stationery expenses |
|---|---|---|---|---|---|---|
| Bal b/f | | 19,546 | | | | |
| T. Hunkin Ltd | | | | | | |
| Victoria Green | | | | | | |
| B. Head Ltd | | | | | | |
| Smiths Ltd | | | | | | |
| Arrow Valley Motor Repairs | | | | | | |
| Total | | | | | | |

There are two cheques from credit customers to be entered into Jo's cash book:

| J Drummond | £623 |
|---|---|
| N Atkinson | £425 |

(b)   **Enter the above details into the debit side of the cash-book below and total each column.**

**Cash-book – debit side**

| Details | Cash | Bank | Receivables |
|---|---|---|---|
| Balance b/f | 986 | | |
| J Drummond | | | |
| N Atkinson | | | |
| Total | | | |

(c)   **Using your answers to (a) and (b) above calculate the cash balance.**

£ 

(d)   **Using your answers to (a) and (b) above calculate the bank balance.**

£ 

(e)   **Will the bank balance calculated in (d) above be a debit or a credit balance?**

Debit/Credit

## 20   CHUGGER LTD

The following transactions all took place on 31 July and have been entered in the credit side of the cash-book as shown below. No entries have yet been made in the ledgers.

**Cash-book – Credit side**

| Date 20XX | Details | VAT £ | Bank £ |
|---|---|---|---|
| 31 July | Stationery | 16 | 96 |
| 31 July | Photocopier repair | 40 | 240 |

(a)   **What will be the entries in the general ledger?**

**General ledger**

| Account name | Amount £ | Debit ✓ | Credit ✓ |
|---|---|---|---|
| | | | |
| | | | |
| | | | |

Picklist: Stationery, Insurance, Repairs, Purchases ledger control, Sales ledger control, VAT

The following transactions all took place on 31 July and have been entered in the debit side of the cash-book as shown below. No entries have yet been made in the ledgers.

**Cash-book – Debit side**

| Date 20XX | Details | Bank £ |
|---|---|---|
| 31 July | Balance b/f | 6,350 |
| 31 July | BBG Ltd | 7,200 |
| 31 July | EFG Ltd | 5,000 |

(b) **What will be the TWO entries in the sales ledger?**

**Sales ledger**

| Account name | Amount £ | Debit ✓ | Credit ✓ |
|---|---|---|---|
| | | | |
| | | | |

Picklist: Balance b/f, Sales ledger control, BBG Ltd, Purchases ledger control, EFG Ltd, Bank

(c) **What will be the entry in the general ledger?**

**General ledger**

| Account name | Amount £ | Debit ✓ | Credit ✓ |
|---|---|---|---|
| | | | |

Picklist: Balance b/f, EFG Ltd Purchase ledger control, Sales ledger control, VAT, Bank, BBG Ltd

## 21 ITALIAN STALLIONS

The following transactions all took place on 31 Jan and have been entered in the credit side of the cash-book of Italian Stallions Ltd as shown below. No entries have yet been made in the ledgers.

**Cash-book – Credit side**

| Date 20XX | Details | VAT £ | Bank £ |
|---|---|---|---|
| 31 Jan | Printer repair | 32 | 192 |
| 31 Jan | Paper | 16 | 96 |

(a)    **What will be the entries in the general ledger?**

**General ledger**

| Account name | Amount £ | Debit ✓ | Credit ✓ |
|---|---|---|---|
|  |  |  |  |
|  |  |  |  |
|  |  |  |  |

Picklist: Repairs, Office supplies, Purchases ledger control, Sales ledger control, VAT

The following transactions all took place on 31 Jan and have been entered in the debit side of the cash-book as shown below. No entries have yet been made in the ledgers.

**Cash-book – Debit side**

| Date 20XX | Details | Bank £ |
|---|---|---|
| 31 Jan | Balance b/f | 5,100 |
| 31 Jan | AAG Ltd | 4,000 |
| 31 Jan | HLG Ltd | 3,000 |

(b)    **What will be the TWO entries in the sales ledger?**

**Sales ledger**

| Account name | Amount £ | Debit ✓ | Credit ✓ |
|---|---|---|---|
|  |  |  |  |
|  |  |  |  |

Picklist: Balance b/f, Sales ledger control, AAG Ltd, Purchases ledger control, HLG Ltd, Bank

(c)    **What will be the entry in the general ledger?**

**General ledger**

| Account name | Amount £ | Debit ✓ | Credit ✓ |
|---|---|---|---|
|  |  |  |  |

Picklist: Balance b/f, EFG Ltd Purchase ledger control, Sales ledger control, VAT, Bank, BBG Ltd

## 22 FRED'S FISH

The following transactions all took place on 31 Dec and have been entered in the debit side of the cash-book as shown below. No entries have yet been made in the ledgers.

**Cash-book – Debit side**

| Date 20XX | Details | Bank £ |
|-----------|---------|--------|
| 31 Dec | Balance b/f | 4,280 |
| 31 Dec | K and D Ltd | 8,200 |

(a) **What will be the entry in the sales ledger?**

**Sales ledger**

| Account name | Amount £ | Debit ✓ | Credit ✓ |
|--------------|----------|---------|----------|
| | | | |

Picklist: Balance b/f, Bank, Purchases ledger control, K and D Ltd, Sales ledger control

(b) **What will be the entry in the general ledger?**

**General ledger**

| Account name | Amount £ | Debit ✓ | Credit ✓ |
|--------------|----------|---------|----------|
| | | | |

Picklist: Balance b/f, Bank, Purchases ledger control, K and D Ltd, Sales ledger control

The following transactions all took place on 31 Dec and have been entered in the credit side of the cash-book as shown below. No entries have yet been made in the ledgers.

**Cash-book – Credit side**

| Date 20XX | Details | VAT £ | Bank £ |
|-----------|---------|-------|--------|
| 31 Dec | Stationery | 20 | 120 |
| 31 Dec | Postage | | 800 |

(c) **What will be the entries in the general ledger?**

**General ledger**

| Account name | Amount £ | Debit ✓ | Credit ✓ |
|--------------|----------|---------|----------|
| | | | |
| | | | |
| | | | |

Picklist: Bank, Postage, Stationery, Purchases ledger control, Sales ledger control, VAT

# PETTY CASH

## 23 HICKORY HOUSE

Hickory House maintains a petty cash book as both a book of prime entry and part of the double entry accounting system. The following transactions all took place on 31 Dec and have been entered in the petty cash-book as shown below. No entries have yet been made in the general ledger.

**Petty cash-book**

| Date 20XX | Details | Amount £ | Date 20XX | Details | Amount £ | VAT £ | Postage £ | Motor expenses £ | Office expenses |
|---|---|---|---|---|---|---|---|---|---|
| 31 Dec | Balance b/f | 210.00 | 31 Dec | Stapler | 6.72 | 1.12 | | | 5.60 |
| 31 Dec | Bank | 90.00 | 31 Dec | Stamps | 15.00 | | 15.00 | | |
| | | | 31 Dec | Parking | 14.88 | 2.48 | | 12.40 | |
| | | | 31 Dec | Stationery | 19.20 | 3.20 | | | 16.00 |
| | | | 31 Dec | Balance c/d | 244.20 | | | | |
| | | 300.00 | | | 300.00 | 6.80 | 15.00 | 12.40 | 21.60 |

**What will be the FIVE entries in the general ledger?**

**General ledger**

| Account name | Amount £ | Debit ✓ | Credit ✓ |
|---|---|---|---|
| | | | |
| | | | |
| | | | |
| | | | |
| | | | |

Picklist: Balance b/f, Balance c/d, Bank, Stationery, Stapler, Motor expenses, Parking, Office expenses, Petty cash-book, Stamps, Postage, VAT

**24    MESSI & CO**

Messi & Co maintains a petty cash book as a book of prime entry; it is not part of the double entry accounting system. The following transactions all took place on 31 Dec and have been entered in the petty cash-book as shown below. No entries have yet been made in the general ledger.

**Petty cash-book**

| Date 20XX | Details | Amount £ | Date 20XX | Details £ | Amount £ | VAT £ | Postage £ | Motor expenses £ | Office expenses £ |
|---|---|---|---|---|---|---|---|---|---|
| 31 Dec | Op balance | 100.00 | 31 Dec | Paper | 27.33 | 4.55 | | | 22.78 |
| | | | 31 Dec | Stamps | 4.50 | | 4.50 | | |
| | | | 31 Dec | Biscuits | 6.60 | 1.10 | | | 5.50 |
| | | | 31 Dec | Parking | 9.60 | 1.60 | | 8.00 | |
| | | | 31 Dec | Cl balance | 51.97 | | | | |
| | | 100.00 | | | 100.00 | 7.25 | 4.50 | 8.00 | 28.28 |

**What will be the FIVE entries in the general ledger?**

**General ledger**

| Account name | Amount £ | Debit ✓ | Credit ✓ |
|---|---|---|---|
| | | | |
| | | | |
| | | | |
| | | | |
| | | | |

Picklist: Balance b/f, Balance c/d, Bank, Motor expenses, Paper, Parking, Petty cash control, Office expenses, Petty cash-book, Stamps, Postage, VAT

## 25 STAVROS

Stavros maintains a petty cash book as both a book of prime entry and part of the double entry accounting system. The following transactions all took place on 31 July and have been entered in the petty cash-book as shown below. No entries have yet been made in the general ledger.

**Petty cash-book**

| Date 20XX | Details | Amount £ | Date 20XX | Details £ | Amount £ | VAT £ | Sundry expenses £ | Business travel £ | Postage |
|---|---|---|---|---|---|---|---|---|---|
| 1 July | Balance b/f | 140 | 31 July | Newsagent | 16.20 | 2.70 | 13.50 | | |
| 31 July | Bank | 110 | 31 July | Tea & Coffee | 60.00 | 10.00 | 50.00 | | |
| | | | 31 July | | 36.96 | 6.16 | | 30.80 | |
| | | | 31 July | Business Travel | 16.00 | | | | 16.00 |
| | | | 31 July | Postage | 120.84 | | | | |
| | | | | Balance c/d | | | | | |
| | | 250.00 | | | 250.00 | 18.86 | 63.50 | 30.80 | 16.00 |

**What will be the FIVE entries in the general ledger?**

**General ledger**

| Account name | Amount £ | Debit ✓ | Credit ✓ |
|---|---|---|---|
| | | | |
| | | | |
| | | | |
| | | | |
| | | | |

Picklist: Postage, Balance c/d, Bank, Fuel, Balance b/f, Motor repair, Sundry expenses, Petty cash-book, VAT, Business Travel

**26   YUMMY CUPCAKES**

Yummy Cupcakes maintains a petty cash book as a book of prime entry; it is not part of the double entry accounting system. The following transactions all took place on 31 July and have been entered in the petty cash-book as shown below. No entries have yet been made in the general ledger.

**Petty cash-book**

| Date 20XX | Details | Amount £ | Date 20XX | Details £ | Amount £ | VAT £ | Sundry expenses £ | Business travel £ | Postage |
|---|---|---|---|---|---|---|---|---|---|
| 1 July | Op balance | 150.00 | 31 July | Parking | 15.00 | 2.50 | | 12.50 | |
| | | | 31 July | Tea & Coffee | 12.00 | 2.00 | 10.00 | | |
| | | | 31 July | Travel | 39.44 | 6.57 | | 32.87 | |
| | | | 31 July | Stamps | 4.00 | | | | 4.00 |
| | | | 31 July | Cl balance | 79.56 | | | | |
| | | 150.00 | | | 150.00 | 11.07 | 10.00 | 45.37 | 4.00 |

**What will be the FIVE entries in the general ledger?**

**General ledger**

| Account name | Amount £ | Debit ✓ | Credit ✓ |
|---|---|---|---|
| | | | |
| | | | |
| | | | |
| | | | |
| | | | |

Picklist: Postage, Balance c/d, Bank, Fuel, Balance b/f, Motor repair, Sundry expenses, Petty cash-book, VAT, Business Travel

### 27    OOH LA!

Ooh La! maintains a petty cash book as both a book of prime entry and part of the double entry accounting system. The following transactions all took place on 31 Jan and have been entered in the petty cash-book as shown below. No entries have yet been made in the general ledger.

**Petty cash-book**

| Date 20XX | Details | Amount £ | Date 20XX | Details £ | Amount £ | VAT £ | Sundry expenses £ | Motor expense £ | Postage |
|---|---|---|---|---|---|---|---|---|---|
| 1 Jan | Balance b/f | 80.00 | 31 Jan | Newsagent | 12.30 | | 12.30 | | |
| 31 Jan | Bank | 70.00 | 31 Jan | Post office | 43.56 | 7.26 | | | 36.30 |
| | | | 31 Jan | Fuel | 20.40 | 3.40 | | 17.00 | |
| | | | 31 Jan | Tea & | 27.30 | 4.55 | 22.75 | | |
| | | | 31 Jan | Coffee | 46.44 | | | | |
| | | | | Balance c/d | | | | | |
| | | 150.00 | | | 150.00 | 15.21 | 35.05 | 17.00 | 36.30 |

**What will be the FIVE entries in the general ledger?**

**General ledger**

| Account name | Amount £ | Debit ✓ | Credit ✓ |
|---|---|---|---|
| | | | |
| | | | |
| | | | |
| | | | |
| | | | |

Picklist: Postage, Balance c/d, Bank, Motor Expense, Balance b/f, Business Travel, Sundry expenses, Petty cash-book, VAT

### 28    QUEEN VIC

Part way through the month the petty cash account had a balance of £145.00. The cash in the petty cash box was checked and the following notes and coins were there.

| Notes and coins | £ |
|---|---|
| 4 × £20 notes | 80.00 |
| 1 × £10 notes | 10.00 |
| 2 × £5 notes | 10.00 |
| 12 × £1 coins | 12.00 |
| 40 × 50p coins | 20.00 |
| 45 × 20p coins | 9.00 |

(a)  **Reconcile the cash amount in the petty cash box with the balance on the petty cash account.**

| | |
|---|---|
| Amount in petty cash box | £ |
| Balance on petty cash account | £ |
| Difference | £ |

At the end of the month the cash in the petty cash box was £27.25

(b)  **Complete the petty cash reimbursement document below to restore the imprest amount of £150.**

| Petty cash reimbursement | |
|---|---|
| Date: 31.07.20XX | |
| Amount required to restore the cash in the petty cash box. | £ |

## 29   THE ARCHES

This is a summary of petty cash payments made by The Arches.

Mick's Motors paid        £20.00 (no VAT)

Stamps paid             £19.00 (no VAT)

Office Essentials paid     £22.00 plus VAT

(a)  **Enter the above transactions, in the order in which they are shown, in the petty cash-book below.**

(b)  **Total the petty cash-book and show the balance carried down.**

**Petty cash-book**

| Debit side | | Credit side | | | | | |
|---|---|---|---|---|---|---|---|
| Details | Amount £ | Details | Amount £ | VAT £ | Postage £ | Travel £ | Stationery £ |
| Balance b/f | 200.00 | | | | | | |
| | | | | | | | |
| | | | | | | | |
| | | | | | | | |
| | | | | | | | |

Picklist: Amount, Balance b/d, Balance c/d, Details, Postage, Stamps, Stationery, Office Essentials, Mick's Motors, VAT, Travel

**30   RAINBOW**

This is a summary of petty cash payments made by Rainbow.

Colin's Cabs paid          £28.00 (no VAT)

Post Office paid           £18.00 (no VAT)

ABC Stationery paid        £32.00 plus VAT

(a)   **Enter the above transactions, in the order in which they are shown, in the petty cash-book below.**

(b)   **Total the petty cash-book and show the balance carried down.**

**Petty cash-book**

| Debit side | | Credit side | | | | | |
|---|---|---|---|---|---|---|---|
| Details | Amount £ | Details | Amount £ | VAT £ | Postage £ | Travel £ | Stationery £ |
| Balance b/f | 100.00 | | | | | | |
| | | | | | | | |
| | | | | | | | |
| | | | | | | | |
| | | | | | | | |

Picklist: Amount, Balance b/d, Balance c/d, Details, Postage, Post Office, Stationery, ABC Stationery, Colin's Cabs, VAT, Travel

**31   SOOTY & SWEEP**

Part way through the month the petty cash account had a balance of £135.00. The cash in the petty cash box was checked and the following notes and coins were there.

| Notes and coins | £ |
|---|---|
| 2 × £20 notes | 40.00 |
| 6 × £10 notes | 60.00 |
| 15 × £1 coins | 15.00 |
| 18 × 50p coins | 9.00 |
| 12 × 20p coins | 2.40 |
| 10 × 10p coins | 1.00 |

(a)  **Reconcile the cash amount in the petty cash box with the balance on the petty cash account.**

| | |
|---|---|
| Amount in petty cash box | £ |
| Balance on petty cash account | £ |
| Difference | £ |

At the end of the month the cash in the petty cash box was £5.00

(b)  **Complete the petty cash reimbursement document below to restore the imprest amount of £250.**

| Petty cash reimbursement | |
|---|---|
| Date: 31.07.20XX | |
| Amount required to restore the cash in the petty cash box. | £ |

## 32   JAWS DENTISTRY

This is a summary of petty cash payments made by Jaws Dentistry.

| | |
|---|---|
| Ace Taxis paid | £26.00 (no VAT) |
| Kate's Couriers | £27.00 (no VAT) |
| Smiths Stationery | £38.00 plus VAT |

(a)  **Enter the above transactions, in the order in which they are shown, in the petty cash-book below.**

(b)  **Total the petty cash-book and show the balance carried down.**

Petty cash-book

| Debit side | | Credit side | | | | | |
|---|---|---|---|---|---|---|---|
| Details | Amount £ | Details | Amount £ | VAT £ | Postage £ | Travel £ | Stationery £ |
| Balance b/f | 225.00 | | | | | | |
| | | | | | | | |
| | | | | | | | |
| | | | | | | | |
| | | | | | | | |

Picklist: Amount, Balance b/d, Balance c/d, Details, Postage, Kate's Couriers, Smiths Stationery, Ace Taxis, Travel, VAT.

## 33 TOM'S TILES

Part way through the month the petty cash account had a balance of £165.52. The cash in the petty cash box was checked and the following notes and coins were there.

| Notes and coins | £ |
|---|---|
| 4 × £20 notes | 80.00 |
| 4 × £10 notes | 40.00 |
| 3 × £5 notes | 15.00 |
| 18 × £1 coins | 18.00 |
| 7 × 50p coins | 3.50 |
| 18 × 20p coins | 3.60 |
| 19 × 10p coins | 1.90 |
| 6 × 2p coins | 0.12 |

(a) **Reconcile the cash amount in the petty cash box with the balance on the petty cash account.**

| Amount in petty cash box | £ |
|---|---|
| Balance on petty cash account | £ |
| Difference | £ |

At the end of the month the cash in the petty cash box was £25.88.

(b) **Complete the petty cash reimbursement document below to restore the imprest amount of £250.00.**

| Petty cash reimbursement | |
|---|---|
| Date: 30.04.20XX | |
| Amount required to restore the cash in petty cash box | £ |

**34   ROCKY RILEY**

This is a summary of petty cash payments made by Rocky Riley.

| | |
|---|---|
| Kath's Kars paid | £32.00 (no VAT) |
| Stamps paid | £25.00 (no VAT) |
| Pauline's Pens paid | £20.00 plus VAT |

(a)   **Enter the above transactions, in the order in which they are shown, in the petty cash-book below.**

(b)   **Total the petty cash-book and show the balance carried down.**

**Petty cash-book**

| Debit side | | Credit side | | | | | |
|---|---|---|---|---|---|---|---|
| Details | Amount £ | Details | Amount £ | VAT £ | Postage £ | Travel £ | Stationery £ |
| Balance b/f | 175.00 | | | | | | |
| | | | | | | | |
| | | | | | | | |
| | | | | | | | |
| | | | | | | | |

Picklist: Amount, Balance b/d, Balance c/d, Details, Postage, Stamps, Stationery, Pauline's Pens, Kath's Kars, Travel, VAT

**35   MHAIRI MOTORS**

Part way through the month the petty cash account had a balance of £110.00. The cash in the petty cash box was checked and the following notes and coins were there.

| Notes and coins | £ |
|---|---|
| 5 × £10 notes | 50.00 |
| 5 × £5 notes | 25.00 |
| 4 × £1 coins | 4.00 |
| 11 × 50p coins | 5.50 |
| 75 × 20p coins | 15.00 |
| 3 × 10p coins | 0.30 |

(a)     **Reconcile the cash amount in the petty cash box with the balance on the petty cash account.**

| | |
|---|---|
| Amount in petty cash box | £ |
| Balance on petty cash account | £ |
| Difference | £ |

At the end of the month the cash in the petty cash box was £8.50

(b)     **Complete the petty cash reimbursement document below to restore the imprest amount of £200.**

| Petty cash reimbursement | |
|---|---|
| Date: 31.07.20XX | |
| Amount required to restore the cash in the petty cash box. | £ |

# DRAFTING AN INITIAL TRIAL BALANCE

### 36     BROOKLYN BOATS

The following two accounts are in the general ledger of Brooklyn Boats at the close of day on 31 Dec.

(a)     **Insert the balance carried down together with date and details.**

(b)     **Insert the totals.**

(c)     **Insert the balance brought down together with date and details.**

**Electricity**

| Date 20XX | Details | Amount £ | Date 20XX | Details £ | Amount £ |
|---|---|---|---|---|---|
| 01 Dec | Balance b/f | 870 | | | |
| 12 Dec | Bank | 350 | | | |
| | **Total** | | | **Total** | |
| | | | | | |

Picklist: Balance b/d, Balance c/d, Bank, Closing balance, Opening balance, Purchases ledger control

**Discounts received**

| Date 20XX | Details | Amount £ | Date 20XX | Details £ | Amount £ |
|---|---|---|---|---|---|
| | | | 1 Dec | Bal b/f | 500 |
| | | | 15 Dec | Purchase ledger control | 100 |
| | **Total** | | | **Total** | |
| | | | | | |

Picklist: Balance b/d, Balance c/d, Bank, Closing balance, Opening balance, Sales ledger control

## 37 WIGGLE POGGLE LTD

The following two accounts are in the general ledger of Wiggle Poggle Ltd at the close of day on 31 July.

(a) **Insert the balance carried down together with date and details.**

(b) **Insert the totals.**

(c) **Insert the balance brought down together with date and details.**

**Discount allowed**

| Date 20XX | Details | Amount £ | Date 20XX | Details £ | Amount £ |
|---|---|---|---|---|---|
| 01 July | Balance b/f | 1,560 | | | |
| 14 July | Sales ledger control account (SLCA) | 480 | | | |
| 16 July | Sales ledger control account (SLCA) | 120 | | | |
| | **Total** | | | **Total** | |
| | | | | | |

Picklist: Balance b/d, Balance c/d, Bank, Closing balance, Opening balance, Sales ledger control

**Interest income**

| Date 20XX | Details | Amount £ | Date 20XX | Details £ | Amount £ |
|---|---|---|---|---|---|
| | | | 01 July | Balance b/f | 320 |
| | | | 28 July | Bank | 80 |
| | Total | | | Total | |
| | | | | | |

Picklist: Balance b/d, Balance c/d, Bank, Closing balance, Opening balance, Sales ledger control

## 38 CRAZY CURTAINS

The following two accounts are in the general ledger of Crazy Curtains at the close of day on 31 Jan.

(a) **Insert the balance carried down together with date and details.**

(b) **Insert the totals.**

(c) **Insert the balance brought down together with date and details.**

**Electricity expense**

| Date 20XX | Details | Amount £ | Date 20XX | Details £ | Amount £ |
|---|---|---|---|---|---|
| 01 Jan | Bal b/f | 200 | | | |
| 22 Jan | Bank | 250 | | | |
| | Total | | | Total | |
| | | | | | |

Picklist: Balance b/d, Balance c/d, Bank, Closing balance, Opening balance, Electricity Expense

**Rental income**

| Date 20XX | Details | Amount £ | Date 20XX | Details £ | Amount £ |
|---|---|---|---|---|---|
| | | | 01 Jan | Balance b/f | 400 |
| | | | 28 Jan | Bank | 600 |
| | Total | | | Total | |
| | | | | | |

Picklist: Balance b/d, Balance c/d, Bank, Closing balance, Opening balance, Sales ledger control

## 39   SMITH & SON

Below is a list of balances to be transferred to the trial balance of Smith & Son at 31 Dec.

**Place the figures in the debit or credit column, as appropriate, and total each column.**

| Account name | Amount £ | Debit £ | Credit £ |
|---|---|---|---|
| Fixtures and fittings | 8,250 | | |
| Capital | 18,400 | | |
| Bank overdraft | 4,870 | | |
| Petty cash control | 350 | | |
| Sales ledger control (SLCA) | 42,870 | | |
| Purchases ledger control (PLCA) | 23,865 | | |
| VAT owed to tax authorities | 10,245 | | |
| Inventory | 9,870 | | |
| Loan from bank | 22,484 | | |
| Sales | 180,264 | | |
| Sales returns | 5,420 | | |
| Purchases | 129,030 | | |
| Purchases returns | 2,678 | | |
| Discount allowed | 2,222 | | |
| Discount received | 3,432 | | |
| Heat and Light | 1,490 | | |
| Motor expenses | 2,354 | | |
| Wages | 42,709 | | |
| Rent and rates | 10,600 | | |
| Repairs | 3,020 | | |
| Hotel expenses | 1,890 | | |
| Telephone | 2,220 | | |
| Delivery costs | 1,276 | | |
| Miscellaneous expenses | 2,667 | | |
| **Totals** | | | |

**40   EXPIALIDOCIOUS LTD**

Below is a list of balances to be transferred to the trial balance of Expialidocious Ltd as at 31 July.

**Place the figures in the debit or credit column, as appropriate, and total each column.**

| Account name | Amount £ | Debit £ | Credit £ |
|---|---|---|---|
| Capital | 25,360 | | |
| Petty cash control | 250 | | |
| Loan from bank | 11,600 | | |
| Sales ledger control (SLCA) | 159,242 | | |
| Purchases ledger control (PLCA) | 83,682 | | |
| Motor vehicles | 35,900 | | |
| Inventory | 28,460 | | |
| Bank overdraft | 10,063 | | |
| VAT owed from tax authorities | 15,980 | | |
| Purchases | 343,014 | | |
| Purchases returns | 1,515 | | |
| Wages | 56,150 | | |
| Motor expenses | 2,950 | | |
| Interest income | 400 | | |
| Sales | 532,900 | | |
| Sales returns | 5,760 | | |
| Stationery | 1,900 | | |
| Light & heat | 6,500 | | |
| Discount received | 200 | | |
| Discount allowed | 2,160 | | |
| Interest paid on overdraft | 550 | | |
| Travel | 1,800 | | |
| Marketing | 650 | | |
| Telephone | 1,510 | | |
| Miscellaneous expenses | 2,944 | | |
| **Totals** | | | |

## 41    DIXON FURNITURE

Below is a list of balances to be transferred to the trial balance of Dixon Furniture as at 31 Jan.

**Place the figures in the debit or credit column, as appropriate, and total each column.**

| Account name | Amount £ | Debit £ | Credit £ |
|---|---|---|---|
| Motor vehicles | 40,100 | | |
| Capital | 35,000 | | |
| Petty cash control | 150 | | |
| Bank balance | 14,654 | | |
| Wages | 37,890 | | |
| Travel expenses | 1,500 | | |
| Rental income | 1,000 | | |
| Sales | 435,600 | | |
| Loan from bank | 10,000 | | |
| Sales ledger control (SLCA) | 127,456 | | |
| Inventory | 22,500 | | |
| Purchases ledger control (PLCA) | 91,250 | | |
| VAT due to tax authorities | 12,500 | | |
| Purchases | 325,600 | | |
| Sales returns | 6,500 | | |
| Purchases returns | 1,250 | | |
| Sundry expenses | 3,600 | | |
| Electricity expense | 450 | | |
| Bank interest received | 360 | | |
| Fuel expense | 900 | | |
| Discount received | 600 | | |
| Discount allowed | 1,560 | | |
| Advertising | 300 | | |
| Telephone | 1,900 | | |
| Miscellaneous expenses | 2,500 | | |
| **Totals** | | | |

# DOCUMENTATION AND RECORDS FOR SUPPLIERS

## 42   NAN NURSING

A supply of chocolate puddings have been delivered to Nan Nursing by Pudding and Co. The purchase order sent from Nan Nursing, and the invoice from Pudding and Co, are shown below.

---

**Nan Nursing**

**22 Nursery Road**

**Keighley, BD22 7BD**

**Purchase Order No. HH72**

**To:** Pudding and Co

**Date:** 15 August 20XX

Please supply 50 chocolate puddings product code 742087

**Purchase price:** £20 per 10, plus VAT

**Discount:** less 10% trade discount, as agreed.

---

**Pudding and Co**

**17 Pudding Lane, Bradford, BD19 7HX**

**VAT Registration No. 234 7654 00**

**Invoice No. 428**

Nan Nursing

22 Nursery Road

Keighley, BD22 7BD

20 August  20XX

| | |
|---|---|
| 50 ........ chocolate puddings product code 742087 @ £2 each | £50 |
| Less Trade Discount | £10 |
| Net | £40 |
| VAT | £ 8 |
| Total | £48 |

Terms: 30 days net

---

**Check the invoice against the purchase order and answer the following questions.**

| | | |
|---|---|---|
| Has the correct purchase price of the chocolate puddings been charged? | Y | N |
| Has the correct total discount been calculated? | Y | N |
| What would be the VAT amount charged if the invoice was correct? | £_____ | |
| What would be the total amount charged if the invoice was correct? | £_____ | |

---

**43    PIXIE PAPERS**

A supply of paper has been delivered to Alpha Ltd by Pixie Paper.  The purchase order sent from Alpha Ltd, and the invoice from Pixie Paper, are shown below.

---

**Alpha Ltd**

**121 Baker St**

**Newcastle, NE1 7DJ**

**Purchase Order No. PO1792**

**To:** Pixie Paper

**Date:** 5 Aug 20XX

Please supply 50 boxes of A4 paper product code 16257

**Purchase price:** £10 per box, plus VAT

**Discount:** less 10% trade discount, as agreed.

---

**Pixie Paper**

**24 Eden Terrace, Durham, DH9 7TE**

**VAT Registration No. 464 392 401**

**Invoice No. 1679**

Alpha Ltd

121 Baker St

Newcastle, NE1 7DJ

9 Aug 20XX

| | |
|---|---|
| 50 boxes of A4 paper,  product code 16257  @ £10 each | £500 |
| VAT | £100 |
| Total | £600 |

**Terms:** 30 days net

---

**Check the invoice against the purchase order and answer the following questions.**

| | | |
|---|---|---|
| Has the correct product been supplied by Pixie Paper? | Y | N |
| Has the correct net price been calculated? | Y | N |
| Has the total invoice price been calculated correctly? | Y | N |
| What would be the VAT amount charged if the invoice was correct? | £____ | |
| What would be the total amount charged if the invoice was correct? | £____ | |

## 44 ALPHA LTD

Shown below is a statement of account received from a credit supplier, and the supplier's account as shown in the purchases ledger of Alpha Ltd.

**ABG Ltd**

**14 Hassle Street, Durham, DH9 7RQ**

**To:** Alpha Ltd

121 Baker St

Newcastle, NE1 7DJ

### STATEMENT OF ACCOUNT

| Date 20XX | Invoice number | Details | Invoice amount £ | Cheque amount £ | Balance £ |
|---|---|---|---|---|---|
| 1 May | 468 | Goods | 7,600 | | 7,600 |
| 1 June | | Cheque | | 2,500 | 5,100 |
| 5 June | 472 | Goods | 4,200 | | 9,300 |
| 12 June | 478 | Goods | 500 | | 9,800 |
| 22 June | 486 | Goods | 1,680 | | 11,480 |
| 30 June | | Cheque | | 2,000 | 9,480 |

**ABG Ltd**

| Date 20XX | Details | Amount £ | Date 20XX | Details | Amount £ |
|---|---|---|---|---|---|
| 4 June | Bank | 2,500 | 3 May | Purchases | 7,600 |
| 28 June | Bank | 2,000 | 8 June | Purchases | 4,200 |
| 28 July | Purchase return | 900 | 15 June | Purchases | 500 |

(a) **Which item is missing from the statement of account from ABG Ltd?**

Picklist: cheque for £2,500, invoice 468, Invoice 472, Purchase return £900, Invoice 486, Cheque for £2,000

(b) **Which item is missing from the supplier account in Alpha Ltd's purchases ledger?**

Picklist: Invoice 468, Invoice 472, Invoice 478, Invoice 486, Purchase return £900, Cheque for £2,500

(c) **Once the omitted items have been recorded, what is the agreed balance outstanding between Alpha Ltd and ABG Ltd?**

£

**45** **MAXIMUS LTD**

Alpha Ltd sends out cheques to suppliers on the last day of the month following the month of invoice. Below is an extract from the purchases ledger of Alpha Ltd.

**Maximus Ltd**

| Date 20XX | Details | Amount £ | Date 20XX | Details | Amount £ |
|---|---|---|---|---|---|
| 15 July | Purchases returns credit note 252 | 964 | 1 July | Balance b/f | 5,980 |
| 21 July | Purchase return credit note 258 | 1,218 | 12 July | Purchases Invoice 864 | 6,386 |
| 31 July | Bank | 5,980 | | | |
| | | | | | |

(a) **Complete the remittance advice note below.**

| Alpha Ltd |
|---|
| 121 Baker St |
| Newcastle, NE1 7DJ |

**REMITTANCE ADVICE**

**To:** Maximus Ltd 20XX                                   **Date:** 31 Aug

Please find attached our cheque in payment of the following amounts.

| Invoice number | Credit note number | Amount £ |
|---|---|---|
| | | |
| | | |
| | | |
| | | |
| | Total amount paid | |

(b) **Are these two statements true or false?**

A remittance note is for our records only                                                    T        F

A remittance note is sent to a supplier to advise them of the amount being paid    T        F

**46    HOLLY LTD**

The account shown below is in the purchase ledger of AD Wholesale.  A cheque for £4,770 has now been paid to this supplier.

**Holly Ltd**

| Date 20XX | Details | Amount £ | Date 20XX | Details | Amount £ |
|---|---|---|---|---|---|
| | | | 5 Jan | Balance b/f | 1,500 |
| 15 Jan | Purchase return 251 | 540 | 19 Jan | Purchase invoice 3658 | 2,360 |
| 31 Jan | Purchase return 286 | 360 | 27 Jan | Purchase invoice 2987 | 1,450 |

(a)    **Which item has been not been included in the payment, causing it to be overstated?**

|  |
|---|

Picklist: Balance b/f, Purchase invoice 3658, Bank, Purchase returns 286, Purchase invoice 2987

An invoice has been received from Rickman Repairs for £860 plus VAT of £172. A prompt payment discount of 10% will be offered for payment within 30 days.

(b)    **What is the amount we should pay, if we meet the 30 days requirement?**

£ |  |

(c)    **How much VAT is payable if the payment is NOT made in 30 days?**

£ |  |

(d)    **What is the amount we should pay if payment is NOT made within 30 days?**

£ |  |

**47    PAINTS R US**

A supply of paint has been delivered to Painting Supplies Ltd by Paints R Us. The purchase order sent from Painting Supplies Ltd, and the invoice from Paints R Us, are shown below.

---

**Painting Supplies Ltd**

**19 Edmund St**

**Newcastle, NE6 5DJ**

**Purchase Order No. PO6548**

**To:** Paints R Us

**Date:** 5 Feb 20XX

Please supply 20 tins of blue paint, product code 23567

**Purchase price:** £8 per tin, plus VAT

**Discount:** less 5% prompt payment discount, as agreed.

---

**Paints R Us**

**19 Valley Gardens, Stanley, DH5 8JJ**

**VAT Registration No. 421 385 602**

**Invoice No. 2485**

Painting Supplies Ltd

19 Edmund St

Newcastle, NE6 5DJ

10 Feb 20XX

| | |
|---|---:|
| 20 tins of blue paint, product code 23567 @ £8 each | £160.00 |
| VAT | £30.00 |
| Total | £190.00 |

**Terms:** 30 days net

---

**Check the invoice against the purchase order and answer the following questions.**

| | | |
|---|---|---|
| Has the correct product been supplied? | Y | N |
| Has the correct net price been calculated? | Y | N |
| Has the total invoice price been calculated correctly? | Y | N |
| What would be the VAT amount charged if the invoice was correct? | £_____ | |
| What would be the total amount charged if the invoice was correct? | £_____ | |

## 48    EP MANUFACTURERS

Shown below is a statement of account received from a credit supplier, and the supplier's account as shown in the purchases ledger of EP Manufacturers.

**KLP Ltd**

**19 Mussell Street, Newcastle, NE4 8JH**

**To:** EP Manufacturers
19 Edmund St
Newcastle, NE6 5DJ

### STATEMENT OF ACCOUNT

| Date 20XX | Invoice number | Details | Invoice amount £ | Cheque amount £ | Balance £ |
|---|---|---|---|---|---|
| 1 Jan | 468 | Goods | 5,200 | | 5,200 |
| 3 Jan | 458 | Goods | 3,600 | | 8,800 |
| 8 Jan | | Cheque | | 1,400 | 7,400 |
| 19 Jan | 478 | Goods | 800 | | 8,200 |
| 21 Jan | | Cheque | | 6,500 | 1,700 |
| 28 Jan | 488 | Goods | 4,350 | | 6,050 |

**KLP Ltd**

| Date 20XX | Details | Amount £ | Date 20XX | Details | Amount £ |
|---|---|---|---|---|---|
| 8 Jan | Bank | 1,400 | 1 Jan | Purchases | 5,200 |
| 21 Jan | Bank | 6,500 | 3 Jan | Purchases | 3,600 |
| 31 Jan | Bank | 1,200 | 19 Jan | Purchases | 800 |

(a)    **Which item is missing from the statement of account from KLP Ltd?**

Picklist: cheque for £1,200, invoice 468, Invoice 478, Cheque for £6,500, Invoice 488, Cheque for £1,400

(b)    **Which item is missing from the supplier account in EP Manufacturers' purchases ledger?**

Picklist: Invoice 468, Invoice 472, Invoice 478, Invoice 488, Purchase return £900, Cheque for £2,500

(c)    **Once the omitted items have been recorded, what is the agreed balance outstanding between EP Manufacturers and KLP Ltd?**

£

**49   STANNY LTD**

Ringo's Rings sends out cheques to suppliers on the last day of the month following the month of invoice. Below is an extract from the purchases ledger of Ringo's Rings.

**Stanny Ltd**

| Date 20XX | Details | Amount £ | Date 20XX | Details | Amount £ |
|---|---|---|---|---|---|
| 13 Feb | Purchases returns credit note 198 | 650 | 1 Feb | Balance b/f | 4,650 |
| 19 Feb | Purchase return credit note 154 | 1,250 | 10 Feb | Purchases Invoice 694 | 2,300 |
| 28 Feb | Bank | 4,650 | 11 Feb | Purchase invoice 658 | 3,640 |
| | | | | | |

(a)   **Complete the remittance advice note below.**

**Ringo Rings**

**37 Parker Lane**

**Stoke SK1 0KE**

**REMITTANCE ADVICE**

**To:** Stanny Ltd                                          **Date:** 31 Mar 20XX

Please find attached our cheque in payment of the following amounts.

| Invoice number | Credit note number | Amount £ |
|---|---|---|
| | | |
| | | |
| | | |
| | | |
| | | |
| **Total amount paid** | | |

(b)   **Are these two statements true or false?**

A remittance note is for ours and the supplier's records                              T    F

A remittance note is sent by a supplier confirming amounts received from them    T    F

## 50   TOYWORLD

Shown below is a statement of account received from a credit supplier, and the supplier's account as shown in the purchases ledger of Hickory House

**Toyworld**

**18 Landview Road**

**Skipton**

**BD27 4TU**

**To:** Hickory House

22 Nursery Road

Keighley, BD22 7BD

**STATEMENT OF ACCOUNT**

| Date 20XX | Invoice number | Details | Invoice amount £ | Cheque amount £ | Balance £ |
|---|---|---|---|---|---|
| 1 Jan | 207 | Goods | 2,500 | | 2,500 |
| 8 April | 310 | Goods | 900 | | 3,400 |
| 9 June | | Cheque | | 3,400 | 0 |
| 17 Aug | 504 | Goods | 500 | | 500 |
| 18 Aug | 505 | Goods | 4,000 | | 4,500 |

**Toyworld**

| Date 20XX | Details | Amount £ | Date 20XX | Details | Amount £ |
|---|---|---|---|---|---|
| 9 June | Bank | 3,400 | 1 Jan | Purchases | 2,500 |
| 25 June | Bank | 500 | 8 April | Purchases | 900 |
| | | | 17 Aug | Purchases | 500 |

(a)   **Which item is missing from the statement of account from Toyworld?**

<br>

Picklist: Invoice 207, Invoice 310, Invoice 504, Invoice 505, Cheque for £3,400, Cheque for £500

(b)   **Which item is missing from the supplier account in Hickory Houses' purchases ledger?**

<br>

Picklist: Invoice 207, Invoice 310, Invoice 504, Invoice 505, Cheque for £3,400, Cheque for £500

(c)   **Assuming any differences between the statement of account from Toyworld and the supplier account in Hickory Houses' purchases ledger are simply due to omission errors, what is the amount owing to Toyworld?**

£

**51 HENRY HOUSE**

Henry House sends out cheques to suppliers on the last day of the month following the month of invoice. Below is an extract from the purchases ledger of Henry House.

**Abbies Party Ltd**

| Date 20XX | Details | Amount £ | Date 20XX | Details | Amount £ |
|---|---|---|---|---|---|
| 17 July | Purchases returns credit note 27 | 82 | 15 July | Purchases Invoice 242 | 220 |
| | | | 10 Aug | Purchases Invoice 764 | 44 |

(a) **Complete the remittance advice note below.**

**Henry House**

**22 Nursery Road**

**Keighley, BD22 7BD**

**REMITTANCE ADVICE**

**To:** Abbies Party

**Date:** 31 August 20XX

Please find attached our cheque in payment of the following amounts.

| Invoice number | Credit note number | Amount £ |
|---|---|---|
| | | |
| | | |
| | | |
| | | |
| **Total amount paid** | | |

(b) **Which of the following statements is true?**

| | | |
|---|---|---|
| The remittance advice note will be sent to the inventory dept to advise them inventory has been paid for | | A |
| The remittance advice note will be sent to the customer to advise them of the amount being paid | | B |
| The remittance advice note will be sent to Henry House's bank to confirm payment is to be made | | C |
| The remittance advice note will be sent to the supplier to advise them of the amount being paid | | D |

## 52    GREY GARAGES

Grey Garages makes payments to suppliers by BACS on the 25th of every month and includes all items that have been outstanding for more than 10 days.

Below is a pre-printed remittance advice slip taken from a statement of account received from a supplier, Mulberry Motors, showing all items outstanding.

**Complete the remittance advice ready for the next payment to Mulberry Motors.**

| Remittance advice | | | | |
|---|---|---|---|---|
| **To:** Mulberry Motors | | | | |
| **From:** Grey Garages | | | | |
| **Payment method:** | | | **Date of payment:** | |
| Items outstanding | | | | Tick if included in payment |
| Date 20XX | Details | Amount £ | | |
| 23-Jun | Invoice 213 | 740 | | |
| 06-Jul | Credit note 14 | 120 | | |
| 13-Jul | Invoice 216 | 620 | | |
| 19-Jul | Invoice 257 | 870 | | |
| | Total amount paid | | £ | |

## 53  ERRICO

The two invoices below were received on 5 June from credit suppliers who offer prompt payment discounts.

**Invoices:**

Giacomo

VAT registration 446 1552 01

Invoice number 1923

To: Errico                                                4 June 20XX

|  | £ |
|---|---|
| 4 product code 45 @ £14.50 each | 58.00 |
| VAT @ 20% | 11.60 |
| | ——— |
| Total | 69.60 |

Terms: 3% prompt payment discount if payment is received within 7 days of the invoice date.

Gaetani

VAT registration 446 4742 01

Invoice number 4578

To: Errico                                                4 June 20XX

|  | £ |
|---|---|
| 3 product code 42a @ £11.50 each | 34.50 |
| VAT @ 20% | 6.90 |
| | ——— |
| Total | 41.40 |

Terms: 5% prompt payment discount if payment is received within 5 days of the invoice date.

Calculate the amount to be paid to each supplier if the prompt payment discount is taken and show the date by which the supplier should receive the payment.

| Supplier | £ | Date by which the payment should be received by the supplier |
|---|---|---|
| Giacomo | | |
| Gaetani | | |

# DOCUMENTATION AND RECORDS FOR CUSTOMERS

**54   ALESSANDRO LTD**

On 1 Aug Alessandro Ltd delivered the following goods to a credit customer, Palermo Wholesale.

| |
|---|
| **Alessandro Ltd**<br>**8 Alan Street**<br>**Glasgow, G1 7DJ**<br><br>Delivery note No. 24369<br>01 Aug 20XX<br><br>Palermo Wholesale                                       **Customer account code:** AGG42<br>17 Zoo Lane<br>Dartford<br>DH8 4TJ<br><br>40 standard baths, product code SB05 |

The list price of the goods was £62.50 each plus VAT. Palermo Wholesale are to be given a 12% trade discount and a 5% discount if they pay within 5 working days.

(a)    **Complete the invoice below.**

**Alessandro Ltd**
**8 Alan Street**
**Glasgow, G1 7DJ**
**VAT Registration No. 398 2774 01**

Palermo Wholesale                                        **Customer account code:**
167 Front St
Stanley
DH8 4TJ
                                                         **Delivery note number:**
                                                         **Date:** 1 Aug 20XX
**Invoice No:** 327

| Quantity | Product code | Total list price £ | Net amount after discount £ | VAT £ | Gross £ |
|---|---|---|---|---|---|
| | | | | | |

Alessandro Ltd offers each customer a discount of 5% if they pay within 30 days.

(b)    **What is the name of this type of discount?**

| |
|---|
| |

Picklist: Bulk discount, prompt payment discount, trade discount

## 55 HLB WHOLESALE

On 1 Feb Painting Supplies Ltd delivered the following goods to a credit customer, HLB Wholesale.

| | |
|---|---|
| **Painting Supplies Ltd** | |
| **19 Edmund St** | |
| **Newcastle, NE6 5DJ** | |

Delivery note No. 46589

01 Feb 20XX

HLB Wholesale                                                    **Customer account code:** HLB24

98 Back St

Consett

DH4 3PD

20 tins of white paint, product code SD19

The list price of the goods was £15 each plus VAT. HLB Wholesale are to be given a 10% trade discount and a 4% discount if they pay within 4 working days.

(a)     **Complete the invoice below.**

**Painting Supplies Ltd**
**19 Edmund St**
**Newcastle, NE6 5DJ**

**VAT Registration No. 402 2958 02**

HLB Wholesale                                           **Customer account code:**
98 Back St
Consett
DH4 3PD

**Date:** 1 Feb 20XX                                      **Delivery note number:**

                                                          **Invoice No:** 298

| Quantity | Product code | Total list price £ | Net amount after discount £ | VAT £ | Gross £ |
|---|---|---|---|---|---|
| | | | | | |

Painting Supplies Ltd offer a discount of 10% if their customers buy from them.

(b)     **What is the name of this type of discount?**

| |
|---|
| |

Picklist: bulk discount, prompt payment discount, trade discount

**56    MASHED LTD**

On 1 Aug Hickory House delivered the following goods to a credit customer, Mashed Ltd.

---

**Hickory House**
**22 Nursery Road**
**Keighley, BD22 7BD**

Delivery note No. 472
01 Aug 20XX

Mashed Ltd                                          **Customer account code:** MA87
42 Moorside Court
Ilkley
Leeds, LS29 4PR

20 flower pots, product code P10

---

The list price of the goods was £5 per flower pot plus VAT.  Mashed Ltd is to be given a 10% trade discount and a 4% early payment discount.

(a)    **Complete the invoice below.**

---

**Hickory House**
**22 Nursery Road**
**Keighley, BD22 7BD**

**VAT Registration No. 476 1397 02**

Mashed Ltd                                          **Customer account code:**
42 Moorside Court
Ilkley
Leeds, LS29 4PR                              **Delivery note number:**

**Date:** 1 Aug 20XX
**Invoice No:** 47

| Quantity of pots | Product code | Total list price £ | Net amount after discount £ | VAT £ | Gross £ |
|---|---|---|---|---|---|
|  |  |  |  |  |  |

---

Hickory House offers each customer a discount if they buy over a certain quantity of goods.

(b)    **What is the name of this type of discount?**

|  |
|---|

Picklist: Bulk discount, prompt payment discount, trade discount

---

**57   WILLIAM & SAMMY LTD**

The account shown below is in the sales ledger of Hickory House.  A cheque for £668 has now been received from this customer.

**William and Sammy Ltd**

| Date 20XX | Details | Amount £ | Date 20XX | Details | Amount £ |
|---|---|---|---|---|---|
| 1 June | Balance b/f | 4,250 | 2 June | Bank | 4,250 |
| 23 June | Sales invoice 255 | 1,876 | 15 June | Sales returns credit note 98 | 1,208 |
| 30 June | Sales Invoice 286 | 2,459 | | | |

(a)   **Which item has not been included in the payment?**

|  |
|---|
|  |

Picklist: Balance b/f, Sales invoice 255, Sales invoice 286, Bank, Sales returns credit note 98

An invoice is being prepared to be sent to William and Sammy Ltd for £3,890 plus VAT of £778.  A prompt payment discount of 4% will be offered for payment within 10 days.

(b)   **What is the amount Hickory House should receive if payment is made within 10 days?**

| £ |
|---|
|  |

(c)   **What is the amount Hickory House should receive if payment is NOT made within 10 days?**

| £ |
|---|
|  |

**58   DIAMONDS & RUBIES LTD**

The following is a summary of transactions with Diamonds & Rubies Ltd, a new credit customer.

| |
|---|
| Invoice 3927, 5 Aug. £4,640 |
| Credit note 96, 10 Aug, £980 |
| Invoice 3964, 21 Aug, £1,560 |
| Credit note 104, 28 Aug, £650 |
| Cheque received, 30 Aug, £2,100 |

**Complete the statement of account below.**

**Stavros**

**121 Baker St**

**Newcastle, NE1 7DJ**

**To:** Diamonds & Rubies Ltd              **Date:** 31 Aug 20XX

| Date 20XX | Details | Transaction amount £ | Outstanding amount £ |
|---|---|---|---|
| 5 Aug | Invoice 3927 | | |
| 10 Aug | Credit note 96 | | |
| 21 Aug | Invoice 3964 | | |
| 28 Aug | Credit note 104 | | |
| 30 Aug | Cheque received | | |

## 59    MAX LTD

The following is a summary of transactions with Max Ltd, a new credit customer of Painting Supplies Ltd.

| |
|---|
| Invoice 4658, 5 Feb. £2,560 |
| Invoice 3964, 11 Feb, £3,290 |
| Credit note 125, 21 Feb, £230 |
| Credit note 139, 23 Feb, £560 |
| Cheque received, 27 Feb, £1,900 |

**Complete the statement of account below.**

**Painting Supplies Ltd**

**19 Edmund St**

**Newcastle, NE6 5DJ**

**To:** Max Ltd                      **Date:** 28 Feb 20XX

| Date 20XX | Details | Transaction amount £ | Outstanding amount £ |
|---|---|---|---|
| 5 Feb | Invoice 4658 | | |
| 11 Feb | Invoice 3964 | | |
| 21 Feb | Credit note 125 | | |
| 23 Feb | Credit note 139 | | |
| 27 Feb | Cheque received | | |

## 60    BETA BOARDS

The following is a summary of transactions with Ava Ltd, a new credit customer of Beta Boards

| |
|---|
| £350 re invoice 222 of 10 Aug |
| Cheque for £225 received 12 Aug |
| £744 re invoice 305 of 15 Aug |
| £339 re credit note 194 on 20 Aug |
| Cheque for £530 received 24 Aug |

**Complete the statement of account below.**

**Beta Boards**

**3 Victoria Avenue**

**Troon**

**KA5 2BD**

**To:** Ava Ltd                                                  **Date:** 31 Aug 20XX

| Date 20XX | Details | Transaction amount £ | Outstanding amount £ |
|---|---|---|---|
| 10 Aug | Invoice 222 | | |
| 12 Aug | Cheque | | |
| 15 Aug | Invoice 305 | | |
| 20 Aug | Credit note 194 | | |
| 24 Aug | Cheque | | |

# UNDERSTANDING THE DOUBLE ENTRY SYSTEM

## 61    ACCOUNTING EQUATION

Financial accounting is based upon the accounting equation.

(a)    **Show whether the following statements are true or false.**

| | | |
|---|---|---|
| Assets less capital is equal to liabilities | True | False |
| Assets plus liabilities are equal to capital | True | False |
| Capital plus liabilities are equal to assets | True | False |

(b)    **Classify each of the following items as an asset or a liability by using the drop down lists.**

| Item | Asset or liability? |
|---|---|
| Inventory | |
| Machinery | |
| 5 year loan | |

## 62    CLASSIFICATION

Classify each of the accounts below by adjoining a line between the account and correct classification.

| Accounts | Classification |
|----------|----------------|
| Payables (PLCA) | Asset |
| Inventory | Income |
| Commission received | Liability |

## 63    FINANCIAL ACCOUNTING

Financial accounting is based upon the accounting equation.

(a)    **Show whether the following statements are true or false.**

| | | |
|---|---|---|
| Capital is equal to assets plus liabilities | True | False |
| Assets less liabilities are equal to capital | True | False |
| Liabilities are equal to capital plus assets | True | False |

(b)    **Classify each of the following items as an asset or a liability.**

| Item | Asset or liability? |
|------|---------------------|
| VAT owed to tax authorities | |
| Amounts owing to payables | |
| Money in the bank | |

## 64    CAPEX

It is important to understand the difference between capital expenditure, revenue expenditure, capital income and revenue income.

**Select one option in each instance below to show whether the item will be capital income, revenue income, capital expenditure or revenue expenditure.**

| Item | Capital income | Revenue income | Capital expenditure | Revenue expenditure |
|------|----------------|----------------|---------------------|---------------------|
| Receipt from sale of motor vehicle | | | | |
| Receipts from credit sales | | | | |
| Purchase of machinery | | | | |
| Payment of electricity bill | | | | |
| Purchase of goods for resale | | | | |

## 65 REVEX

It is important to understand the difference between capital expenditure, revenue expenditure, capital income and revenue income.

**Select one option in each instance below to show whether the item will be capital income, revenue income, capital expenditure or revenue expenditure.**

| Item | Capital income | Revenue income | Capital expenditure | Revenue expenditure |
|---|---|---|---|---|
| Receipt from sale of machinery | | | | |
| Payment of telephone bill | | | | |
| Purchase of building | | | | |
| Receipts from cash sales | | | | |
| Receipts from receivables | | | | |

## 66 EXPENDITURE TYPES

It is important to understand the difference between capital expenditure, revenue expenditure, capital income and revenue income.

**Select one option in each instance below to show whether the item will be capital expenditure, revenue expenditure, capital income or revenue income.**

| Item | Capital expenditure | Revenue expenditure | Capital income | Revenue income |
|---|---|---|---|---|
| Purchase of a new computer system | | | | |
| Receipts from customers | | | | |
| Receipt from sale of fixtures and fittings | | | | |
| Payments of salaries to staff | | | | |
| Purchase of cleaning materials | | | | |
| Receipt of bank interest | | | | |

**67    ASSET OR LIABILITY**

(a)    **Classify each of the following items as an asset or a liability by using the drop down lists.**

| Item | Asset or liability? |
|---|---|
| Factory building | |
| Money due to suppliers | |
| Car used in business | |

ABC Co has paid an electricity bill by cheque.

(b)    **Complete the sentence below by selecting the correct option to show how this transaction will affect the accounts of ABC Co.**

The expense electricity will *increase/decrease*, the asset of bank will *increase/ decrease*.

**68    ACCOUNTING EQUATION 2**

Show the accounting equation by inserting the appropriate figures using the information provided below:

Note: all figures should be shown as a positive balance.

| Assets and liabilities | £ |
|---|---|
| Land & buildings | 120,000 |
| Cars & machinery | 20,960 |
| Amounts due from credit customers | 4,900 |
| Bank | 12,500 |
| Amounts due to credit suppliers | 13,870 |
| Loan | 15,000 |

| Assets £ | Liabilities £ | Capital £ |
|---|---|---|
| | | |

# Section 2

# ANSWERS TO PRACTICE QUESTIONS

## MAKING ENTRIES IN DAY BOOKS

**1    SDB**

**Sales day-book**

| Date 20XX | Details | Invoice number | Total £ | VAT £ | Net £ | Sales type 1 £ | Sales type 2 £ |
|---|---|---|---|---|---|---|---|
| 31 Dec | Poonams | 105 | 3,600 | 600 | 3,000 | | 3,000 |
| 31 Dec | D. Taylor | 106 | 7,680 | 1,280 | 6,400 | 6,400 | |
| 31 Dec | Smiths | 107 | 3,840 | 640 | 3,200 | | 3,200 |
| | Totals | | 15,120 | 2,520 | 12,600 | 6,400 | 6,200 |

**2    FREDDIE LTD**

**Purchases day-book**

| Date 20XX | Details | Invoice number | Total £ | VAT £ | Net £ | Product 14211 £ | Product 14212 £ |
|---|---|---|---|---|---|---|---|
| 31 July | Box Ltd | 2177 | 960 | 160 | 800 | 800 | |
| 31 July | Shrew Ltd | 2175 | 14,400 | 2,400 | 12,000 | 12,000 | |
| 31 July | Novot & Co | 2176 | 4,800 | 800 | 4,000 | | 4,000 |
| | Totals | | 20,160 | 3,360 | 16,800 | 12,800 | 4,000 |

**3    MAHINDRA LTD**

**Sales day-book**

| Date 20XX | Details | Invoice number | Total £ | VAT £ | Net £ | Sales type 1 £ | Sales type 2 £ |
|---|---|---|---|---|---|---|---|
| 31 Jan | Square Ltd | 3567 | 1,200 | 200 | 1,000 | 1,000 | |
| 31 Jan | Oval & Co | 3568 | 9,600 | 1,600 | 8,000 | | 8,000 |
| 31 Jan | Diamond Ltd | 3569 | 13,200 | 2,200 | 11,000 | | 11,000 |
| 31 Jan | Triangle Ltd | 3570 | 7,920 | 1,320 | 6,600 | 6,600 | |
| | Totals | | 31,920 | 5,320 | 26,600 | 7,600 | 19,000 |

## CODING

### 4    LEO LTD

(a)

| General ledger code | GL530 |
|---|---|
| Supplier account code | DEF14 |

(b)

| To help trace orders and amounts due from particular customers |
|---|

### 5    ELLA'S PAINTS

(a)

| General ledger code | GL395 |
|---|---|
| Supplier account code | MEG20 |

(b)

| To help trace orders and amounts due to particular suppliers |
|---|

### 6    ROBERTO & CO

(a)

| Supplier account code | ALE1 |
|---|---|
| General ledger code | GL72 |

(b)

| To help calculate expense incurred in a GL account |
|---|

## TRANSFERRING DATA FROM DAY BOOKS TO LEDGERS

### 7    LADY LTD

**General ledger**

**Purchases ledger control account**

| | £ | | | £ |
|---|---|---|---|---|
| | | 1 Dec Balance b/d | | 5,103.90 |
| | | **18 Dec Purchases & Vat** | | **903.23** |

**VAT account**

| | £ | | | £ |
|---|---|---|---|---|
| | | 1 Dec Balance b/d | | 526.90 |
| **18 Dec PLCA** | **150.53** | | | |

### Purchases account

| | £ | | £ |
|---|---|---|---|
| 1 Dec Balance b/d | 22,379.52 | | |
| **18 Dec PLCA** | **752.70** | | |

**Subsidiary ledger**

### M Brown

| | £ | | £ |
|---|---|---|---|
| | | 1 Dec Balance b/d | 68.50 |
| | | **1 Dec PDB** | **300.00** |

### H Madden

| | £ | | £ |
|---|---|---|---|
| | | 1 Dec Balance b/d | 286.97 |
| | | **5 Dec PDB** | **183.55** |

### L Singh

| | £ | | £ |
|---|---|---|---|
| | | 1 Dec Balance b/d | 125.89 |
| | | **7 Dec PDB** | **132.60** |

### A Stevens

| | £ | | £ |
|---|---|---|---|
| | | 1 Dec Balance b/d | 12.36 |
| | | **10 Dec PDB** | **90.00** |

### N Shema

| | £ | | £ |
|---|---|---|---|
| | | 1 Dec Balance b/d | 168.70 |
| | | **18 Dec PDB** | **197.08** |

**8     BUTTONS LTD**

(a)     What will be the entries in the purchases ledger?

| Account name | Amount £ | Debit ✓ | Credit ✓ |
|---|---|---|---|
| Peak & Co | 6,240 | | ✓ |
| Max Ltd | 12,720 | | ✓ |
| McIntyre Wholesale | 5,760 | | ✓ |
| Pigmy Ltd | 3,744 | | ✓ |

(b)     What will be the entries in the general ledger?

| Account name | Amount £ | Debit ✓ | Credit ✓ |
|---|---|---|---|
| Purchases | 23,720 | ✓ | |
| VAT | 4,744 | ✓ | |
| Purchase ledger control | 28,464 | | ✓ |

**9     SPARKY LTD**

(a)     What will be the entries in the sales ledger?

**Sales ledger**

| Account name | Amount £ | Debit ✓ | Credit ✓ |
|---|---|---|---|
| Clarkson Ltd | 1,680 | | ✓ |
| Kyle & Co | 720 | | ✓ |

(b)     What will be the entries in the general ledger?

**General ledger**

| Account name | Amount £ | Debit ✓ | Credit ✓ |
|---|---|---|---|
| Sales ledger control account | 2,400 | | ✓ |
| Sales returns | 2,000 | ✓ | |
| VAT | 400 | ✓ | |

## 10    LOUIS LTD

(a)    What will be the entries in the sales ledger?

| Account name | Amount £ | Debit ✓ | Credit ✓ |
|---|---|---|---|
| Sheep & Co | 3,840 | ✓ | |
| Cow Ltd | 11,760 | ✓ | |
| Chicken & Partners | 6,720 | ✓ | |
| Pig Ltd | 14,496 | ✓ | |

(b)    What will be the entries in the general ledger?

| Account name | Amount £ | Debit ✓ | Credit ✓ |
|---|---|---|---|
| Sales ledger control | 36,816 | ✓ | |
| VAT | 6,136 | | ✓ |
| Sales | 30,680 | | ✓ |

## 11    THOMAS & TILLY

(a)    What will be the entries in the purchase ledger?

**Purchases ledger**

| Account name | Amount £ | Debit ✓ | Credit ✓ |
|---|---|---|---|
| May Ltd | 1,920 | ✓ | |
| Hammond & Co | 1,200 | ✓ | |

(b)    What will be the entries in the general ledger?

**General ledger**

| Account name | Amount £ | Debit ✓ | Credit ✓ |
|---|---|---|---|
| Purchase ledger control account | 3,120 | ✓ | |
| Purchase returns | 2,600 | | ✓ |
| VAT | 520 | | ✓ |

## 12   FINCH'S

(a)   What will be the entries in the sales ledger?

| Account name | Amount £ | Debit ✓ | Credit ✓ |
|---|---|---|---|
| Lou and Phil's | 5,040 | ✓ | |
| Eddie and Co | 10,560 | ✓ | |
| Noah's Arc | 2,880 | ✓ | |
| Alex and Freddie | 720 | ✓ | |

(b)   What will be the entries in the general ledger?

| Account name | Amount £ | Debit ✓ | Credit ✓ |
|---|---|---|---|
| Sales | 16,000 | | ✓ |
| VAT | 3,200 | | ✓ |
| Sales ledger control | 19,200 | ✓ | |

## 13   JESSICA & CO

(a)   What will be the entries in the purchases ledger?

**Purchases ledger**

| Account name | Amount £ | Debit ✓ | Credit ✓ |
|---|---|---|---|
| Iona Ltd | 1,680 | ✓ | |
| Matilda Ltd | 4,320 | ✓ | |

(b)   What will be the entries in the general ledger?

**General ledger**

| Account name | Amount £ | Debit ✓ | Credit ✓ |
|---|---|---|---|
| Purchases ledger control account | 6,000 | ✓ | |
| Purchases returns | 5,000 | | ✓ |
| VAT | 1,000 | | ✓ |

## 14    HORSEY REACH

(a)

| Account name | Amount £ | Debit ✓ | Credit ✓ |
|---|---|---|---|
| Sales ledger control | 226.80 | | ✓ |
| VAT | 37.80 | ✓ | |
| Discounts allowed | 189.00 | ✓ | |

(b)

| Account name | Amount £ | Debit ✓ | Credit ✓ |
|---|---|---|---|
| Ashleigh Buildings | 36.00 | | ✓ |
| 143 WGT | 54.00 | | ✓ |
| McDuff McGregor | 43.20 | | ✓ |
| Cameron Travel | 93.60 | | ✓ |

## 15    BUTTERFLY BEES

(a)

| Account name | Amount £ | Debit ✓ | Credit ✓ |
|---|---|---|---|
| Discounts received | 356.00 | | ✓ |
| VAT | 71.20 | | ✓ |
| PLCA | 427.20 | ✓ | |

(b)

| Account name | Amount £ | Debit ✓ | Credit ✓ |
|---|---|---|---|
| Bella Bumps | 24.00 | ✓ | |

**16    OLIVIA ROSE BRIAL SUPPLIES**

(a)

| Account name | Amount £ | Debit ✓ | Credit ✓ |
|---|---|---|---|
| Discounts allowed | 189.00 | ✓ | |
| VAT | 37.80 | ✓ | |
| SLCA | 226.80 | | ✓ |

(b)

| Account name | Amount £ | Debit ✓ | Credit ✓ |
|---|---|---|---|
| Bridezilla | 54.00 | | ✓ |

# THE CASH BOOK

**17    ABC LTD**

(a)    **Cash-book – credit side**

| Details | Cash | Bank | VAT | Payables | Cash purchases | Repairs and renewals |
|---|---|---|---|---|---|---|
| Balance b/f | | | | | | |
| S. Lampard | 216 | | 36 | | 180 | |
| S. Bobbins | 264 | | 44 | | 220 | |
| Penny Rhodes | 530 | | | | 530 | |
| Henley's Ltd | | 4,925 | | 4,925 | | |
| Epic Equipment Maintenance | | 480 | 80 | | | 400 |
| **Total** | 1,010 | 5,405 | 160 | 4,925 | 930 | 400 |

(b)    **Cash book – debit side**

| Details | Cash | Bank | Receivables |
|---|---|---|---|
| Balance b/f | 1,550 | 7,425 | |
| D. Davies | | 851 | 851 |
| E. Denholm | | 450 | 450 |
| **Total** | 1,550 | 8,726 | 1,301 |

(c)    £540

(d)    £3,321

(e)    Debit

## 18   BEDS

(a)   **Cash-book – credit side**

| Details | Cash | Bank | VAT | Payables | Cash purchases | Repairs and renewals |
|---|---|---|---|---|---|---|
| Balance b/f | | | | | | |
| A. Blighty Ltd | 708 | | 118 | | 590 | |
| R Bromby | 228 | | 38 | | 190 | |
| Roxy Bland | 230 | | | | 230 | |
| Burgess Ltd | | 2,400 | | 2,400 | | |
| Fast Equipment Repairs | | 96 | 16 | | | 80 |
| **Total** | 1,166 | 2,496 | 172 | 2,400 | 1,010 | 80 |

(b)   **Cash book – debit side**

| Details | Cash | Bank | Receivables |
|---|---|---|---|
| Balance b/f | 1,175 | 3,825 | |
| A Barnett | | 698 | 698 |
| H Connelly | | 250 | 250 |
| **Total** | 1,175 | 4,773 | 948 |

(c)   £9

(d)   £2,277

(e)   Debit

**19    JO'S**

(a)

| Details | Cash | Bank | VAT | Payables | Cash purchases | Stationery expenses |
|---|---|---|---|---|---|---|
| Bal b/f | | 19,546 | | | | |
| T. Hunkin Ltd | 48 | | 8 | | 40 | |
| Victoria Green | 96 | | 16 | | 80 | |
| B. Head Ltd | 455 | | | | 455 | |
| Smiths Ltd | | 4,250 | | 4,250 | | |
| Arrow Valley Motor Repairs | | 120 | 20 | | | 100 |
| **Total** | 599 | 23,916 | 44 | 4,250 | 575 | 100 |

(b)

| Details | Cash | Bank | Receivables |
|---|---|---|---|
| Balance b/f | 986 | | |
| J Drummond | | 623 | 623 |
| N Atkinson | | 425 | 425 |
| **Total** | 986 | 1,048 | 1,048 |

(c)    £387

(d)    £22,868

(e)    Credit

**20 CHUGGER LTD**

(a) **General ledger**

| Account name | Amount £ | Debit ✓ | Credit ✓ |
|---|---|---|---|
| Stationery expense | 80 | ✓ | |
| Repairs | 200 | ✓ | |
| VAT | 56 | ✓ | |

(b) **Sales ledger**

| Account name | Amount £ | Debit ✓ | Credit ✓ |
|---|---|---|---|
| BBG Ltd | 7,200 | | ✓ |
| EFG Ltd | 5,000 | | ✓ |

(c) **General ledger**

| Account name | Amount £ | Debit ✓ | Credit ✓ |
|---|---|---|---|
| Sales ledger control | 12,200 | | ✓ |

**21 ITALIAN STALLIONS**

(a) **General ledger**

| Account name | Amount £ | Debit ✓ | Credit ✓ |
|---|---|---|---|
| Office supplies | 80 | ✓ | |
| Repairs | 160 | ✓ | |
| VAT | 48 | ✓ | |

(b) **Sales ledger**

| Account name | Amount £ | Debit ✓ | Credit ✓ |
|---|---|---|---|
| AAG Ltd | 4,000 | | ✓ |
| HLG Ltd | 3,000 | | ✓ |

(c) **General ledger**

| Account name | Amount £ | Debit ✓ | Credit ✓ |
|---|---|---|---|
| Sales ledger control | 7,000 | | ✓ |

**22   FRED'S FISH**

(a)   **Sales ledger**

| Account name | Amount £ | Debit ✓ | Credit ✓ |
|---|---|---|---|
| K and D Ltd | 8,200 | | ✓ |

(b)   **General ledger**

| Account name | Amount £ | Debit ✓ | Credit ✓ |
|---|---|---|---|
| Sales ledger control | 8,200 | | ✓ |

(c)   **General ledger**

| Account name | Amount £ | Debit ✓ | Credit ✓ |
|---|---|---|---|
| Stationery | 100 | ✓ | |
| VAT | 20 | ✓ | |
| Postage | 800 | ✓ | |

# PETTY CASH

**23   HICKORY HOUSE**

**General ledger**

| Account name | Amount £ | Debit ✓ | Credit ✓ |
|---|---|---|---|
| VAT | 6.80 | ✓ | |
| Postage | 15.00 | ✓ | |
| Motor expenses | 12.40 | ✓ | |
| Office expenses | 21.60 | ✓ | |
| Bank | 90 | | ✓ |

## 24 MESSI & CO

**General ledger**

| Account name | Amount £ | Debit ✓ | Credit ✓ |
|---|---|---|---|
| VAT | 7.25 | ✓ | |
| Postage | 4.50 | ✓ | |
| Motor expenses | 8.00 | ✓ | |
| Office expenses | 28.28 | ✓ | |
| Petty cash control | 48.03 | | ✓ |

## 25 STAVROS

**General ledger**

| Account name | Amount £ | Debit ✓ | Credit ✓ |
|---|---|---|---|
| VAT | 18.86 | ✓ | |
| Postage | 16.00 | ✓ | |
| Business travel | 30.80 | ✓ | |
| Sundry expenses | 63.50 | ✓ | |
| Bank | 110.00 | | ✓ |

## 26 YUMMY CUPCAKES

**General ledger**

| Account name | Amount £ | Debit ✓ | Credit ✓ |
|---|---|---|---|
| VAT | 11.07 | ✓ | |
| Sundry expenses | 10.00 | ✓ | |
| Business travel | 45.37 | ✓ | |
| Postage | 4.00 | ✓ | |
| Petty cash control | 70.44 | | ✓ |

### 27 OOH LA!

**General ledger**

| Account name | Amount £ | Debit ✓ | Credit ✓ |
|---|---|---|---|
| VAT | 15.21 | ✓ | |
| Postage | 36.30 | ✓ | |
| Sundry expenses | 35.05 | ✓ | |
| Motor expenses | 17.00 | ✓ | |
| Bank | 70.00 | | ✓ |

### 28 QUEEN VIC

(a)

| | |
|---|---|
| Amount in petty cash box | **£141.00** |
| Balance on petty cash account | **£145.00** |
| Difference | **£4.00** |

(b)

| Petty cash reimbursement | |
|---|---|
| **Date:** 31.07.20XX | |
| Amount required to restore the cash in the petty cash box. | **£122.75** |

### 29 THE ARCHES

(a) – (b)

**Petty cash-book**

| Debit side | | Credit side | | | | | |
|---|---|---|---|---|---|---|---|
| Details | Amount £ | Details | Amount £ | VAT £ | Postage £ | Travel £ | Stationery £ |
| Balance b/f | 200.00 | Mick's Motors | 20.00 | | | 20.00 | |
| | | Stamps | 19.00 | | 19.00 | | |
| | | Office Essentials | 26.40 | 4.40 | | | 22.00 |
| | | Balance c/d | 134.60 | | | | |
| | 200.00 | | 200.00 | 4.40 | 19.00 | 20.00 | 22.00 |

## 30    RAINBOW

(a) – (b)

**Petty cash-book**

| Debit side | | Credit side | | | | | |
|---|---|---|---|---|---|---|---|
| Details | Amount £ | Details | Amount £ | VAT £ | Postage £ | Travel £ | Stationery £ |
| Balance b/f | 100.00 | Colin's Cabs | 28.00 | | | 28.00 | |
| | | Post Office | 18.00 | | 18.00 | | |
| | | ABC Stationery | 38.40 | 6.40 | | | 32.00 |
| | | Balance c/d | 15.60 | | | | |
| | 100.00 | | 100.00 | 6.40 | 18.00 | 28.00 | 32.00 |

## 31    SOOTY & SWEEP

(a)

| | |
|---|---|
| Amount in petty cash box | **£127.40** |
| Balance on petty cash account | **£135.00** |
| Difference | **£7.60** |

(b)

| **Petty cash reimbursement** | |
|---|---|
| **Date:** 31.07.20XX | |
| Amount required to restore the cash in the petty cash box. | **£245.00** |

## 32    JAWS DENTISTRY

(a) – (b)

**Petty cash-book**

| Debit side | | Credit side | | | | | |
|---|---|---|---|---|---|---|---|
| Details | Amount £ | Details | Amount £ | VAT £ | Postage £ | Travel £ | Stationery £ |
| Balance b/f | 225.00 | Ace Taxis | 26.00 | | | 26.00 | |
| | | Kate's Couriers | 27.00 | | 27.00 | | |
| | | Smiths Stationery | 45.60 | 7.60 | | | 38.00 |
| | | Balance c/d | 126.40 | | | | |
| | 225.00 | | 225.00 | 7.60 | 27.00 | 26.00 | 38.00 |

**33    TOM'S TILES**

(a)

| | |
|---|---|
| Amount in petty cash box | **£162.12** |
| Balance on petty cash account | **£165.52** |
| Difference | **£3.40** |

(b)

| Petty cash reimbursement | |
|---|---|
| **Date:**  30.04.20XX | |
| Amount required to restore the cash in petty cash box | **£224.12** |

**34    ROCKY RILEY**

(a) – (b)

**Petty cash-book**

| Debit side | | Credit side | | | | | |
|---|---|---|---|---|---|---|---|
| Details | Amount £ | Details | Amount £ | VAT £ | Postage £ | Travel £ | Stationery £ |
| Balance b/f | 175.00 | Kath's Kars | 32.00 | | | 32.00 | |
| | | Stamps | 25.00 | | 25.00 | | |
| | | Pauline's Pens | 24.00 | 4.00 | | | 20.00 |
| | | Balance c/d | 94.00 | | | | |
| | 175.00 | | 175.00 | 4.00 | 25.00 | 32.00 | 20.00 |

**35    MHAIRI MOTORS**

(a)

| | |
|---|---|
| Amount in petty cash box | **£99.80** |
| Balance on petty cash account | **£110.00** |
| Difference | **£10.20** |

(b)

| Petty cash reimbursement | |
|---|---|
| **Date:** 31.07.20XX | |
| Amount required to restore the cash in the petty cash box. | **£191.50** |

# DRAFTING AN INITIAL TRIAL BALANCE

## 36   BROOKLYN BOATS

### Telephone

| Date 20XX | Details | Amount £ | Date 20XX | Details | Amount £ |
|---|---|---|---|---|---|
| 01 Dec | Balance b/f | 870 | 31 Dec | Balance c/d | 1,220 |
| 12 Dec | Bank | 350 | | | |
| | **Total** | 1,220 | | **Total** | 1,220 |
| 1 Jan | Balance b/d | 1,220 | | | |

### Discounts received

| Date 20XX | Details | Amount £ | Date 20XX | Details | Amount £ |
|---|---|---|---|---|---|
| 31 Dec | Balance c/d | 600 | 1 Dec | Balance b/f | 500 |
| | | | 15 Dec | Purchase Ledger control | 100 |
| | **Total** | 600 | | **Total** | 600 |
| | | | 1 Jan | Balance b/d | 600 |

## 37 WIGGLE POGGLE LTD

### Discount allowed

| Date 20XX | Details | Amount £ | Date 20XX | Details | Amount £ |
|---|---|---|---|---|---|
| 01 July | Balance b/f | 1,560 | 31 July | Balance c/d | 2,160 |
| 14 July | Sales ledger control account (SLCA) | 480 | | | |
| | Sales ledger control account (SLCA) | 120 | | | |
| | **Total** | 2,160 | | **Total** | 2,160 |
| 1 Aug | Balance b/d | 2,160 | | | |

### Interest income

| Date 20XX | Details | Amount £ | Date 20XX | Details | Amount £ |
|---|---|---|---|---|---|
| 31 July | Balance c/d | 400 | 01 July | Balance b/f | 320 |
| | | | 28 July | Bank | 80 |
| | **Total** | 400 | | **Total** | 400 |
| | | | 1 Aug | Balance b/d | 400 |

## 38 CRAZY CURTAINS

### Electricity expense

| Date 20XX | Details | Amount £ | Date 20XX | Details | Amount £ |
|---|---|---|---|---|---|
| 01 Jan | Bal b/f | 200 | 31 Jan | Balance c/d | 450 |
| 22 Jan | Bank | 250 | | | |
| | **Total** | 450 | | **Total** | 450 |
| 1 Feb | Balance b/d | 450 | | | |

### Rental income

| Date 20XX | Details | Amount £ | Date 20XX | Details | Amount £ |
|---|---|---|---|---|---|
| 31 Jan | Balance c/d | 1,000 | 01 Jan | Balance b/f | 400 |
| | | | 28 Jan | Bank | 600 |
| | **Total** | 1,000 | | **Total** | 1,000 |
| | | | 1 Feb | Balance b/d | 1,000 |

## 39 SMITH & SON

| Account name | Amount £ | Debit £ | Credit £ |
|---|---|---|---|
| Fixtures and fittings | 8,250 | 8,250 | |
| Capital | 18,400 | | 18,400 |
| Bank overdraft | 4,870 | | 4,870 |
| Petty cash control | 350 | 350 | |
| Sales ledger control (SLCA) | 42,870 | 42,870 | |
| Purchases ledger control (PLCA) | 23,865 | | 23,865 |
| VAT owed to tax authorities | 10,245 | | 10,245 |
| Inventory | 9,870 | 9,870 | |
| Loan from bank | 22,484 | | 22,484 |
| Sales | 180,264 | | 180,264 |
| Sales returns | 5,420 | 5,420 | |
| Purchases | 129,030 | 129,030 | |
| Purchases returns | 2,678 | | 2,678 |
| Discount allowed | 2,222 | 2,222 | |
| Discount received | 3,432 | | 3,432 |
| Heat and light | 1,490 | 1,490 | |
| Motor expenses | 2,354 | 2,354 | |
| Wages | 42,709 | 42,709 | |
| Rent and rates | 10,600 | 10,600 | |
| Repairs | 3,020 | 3,020 | |
| Hotel expenses | 1,890 | 1,890 | |
| Telephone | 2,220 | 2,220 | |
| Delivery costs | 1,276 | 1,276 | |
| Miscellaneous expenses | 2,667 | 2,667 | |
| **Totals** | 532,476 | 266,238 | 266,238 |

**40    EXPIALIDOCIOUS LTD**

| Account name | Amount £ | Debit £ | Credit £ |
|---|---|---|---|
| Capital | 25,360 | | 25,360 |
| Petty cash control | 250 | 250 | |
| Loan from bank | 11,600 | | 11,600 |
| Sales ledger control (SLCA) | 159,242 | 159,242 | |
| Purchases ledger control (PLCA) | 83,682 | | 83,682 |
| Motor vehicles | 35,900 | 35,900 | |
| Inventory | 28,460 | 28,460 | |
| Bank overdraft | 10,063 | | 10,063 |
| VAT owing from tax authorities | 15,980 | 15,980 | |
| Purchases | 343,014 | 343,014 | |
| Purchases returns | 1,515 | | 1,515 |
| Wages | 56,150 | 56,150 | |
| Motor expenses | 2,950 | 2,950 | |
| Interest income | 400 | | 400 |
| Sales | 532,900 | | 532,900 |
| Sales returns | 5,760 | 5,760 | |
| Stationery | 1,900 | 1,900 | |
| Light & heat | 6,500 | 6,500 | |
| Discount received | 200 | | 200 |
| Discount allowed | 2,160 | 2,160 | |
| Interest paid on overdraft | 550 | 550 | |
| Travel | 1,800 | 1,800 | |
| Marketing | 650 | 650 | |
| Telephone | 1,510 | 1,510 | |
| Miscellaneous expenses | 2,944 | 2,944 | |
| **Totals** | | 665,720 | 665,720 |

## 41 DIXON FURNITURE

| Account name | Amount £ | Debit £ | Credit £ |
|---|---|---|---|
| Motor vehicles | 40,100 | 40,100 | |
| Capital | 35,000 | | 35,000 |
| Petty cash control | 150 | 150 | |
| Bank balance | 14,654 | 14,654 | |
| Wages | 37,890 | 37,890 | |
| Travel expenses | 1,500 | 1,500 | |
| Rental income | 1,000 | | 1,000 |
| Sales | 435,600 | | 435,600 |
| Loan from bank | 10,000 | | 10,000 |
| Sales ledger control (SLCA) | 127,456 | 127,456 | |
| Inventory | 22,500 | 22,500 | |
| Purchases ledger control (PLCA) | 91,250 | | 91,250 |
| VAT due to tax authorities | 12,500 | | 12,500 |
| Purchases | 325,600 | 325,600 | |
| Sales returns | 6,500 | 6,500 | |
| Purchases returns | 1,250 | | 1,250 |
| Sundry expenses | 3,600 | 3,600 | |
| Electricity expense | 450 | 450 | |
| Bank interest received | 360 | | 360 |
| Fuel expense | 900 | 900 | |
| Discount received | 600 | | 600 |
| Discount allowed | 1,560 | 1,560 | |
| Advertising | 300 | 300 | |
| Telephone | 1,900 | 1,900 | |
| Miscellaneous expenses | 2,500 | 2,500 | |
| **Totals** | | 587,560 | 587,560 |

# DOCUMENTATION AND RECORDS FOR SUPPLIERS

### 42    NAN NURSING

| | |
|---|---:|
| Has the correct purchase price of the chocolate puddings been charged on the invoice? | N |
| Has the correct discount been applied? | Y |
| What would be the VAT amount charged if the invoice was correct? | £18.00 |
| What would be the total amount charged if the invoice was correct? | £108.00 |

### 43    PIXIE PAPERS

| | |
|---|---:|
| Has the correct product been supplied by Pixie Paper? | Y |
| Has the correct net price been calculated? | N see N1 |
| Has the total invoice price been calculated correctly? | N |
| What would be the VAT amount charged if the invoice was correct? | £90.00 |
| What would be the total amount charged if the invoice was correct? | £540.00 |

N1 – the trade discount of 10% should have been deducted so that the net price was £450.

VAT @ 20% on the net price of £450 is then calculated as £90.00.

### 44    ALPHA LTD

(a)

| Purchase return £900 |
|---|

(b)

| Invoice 486 |
|---|

(c)

| £8,580.00 |
|---|

**45    MAXIMUS LTD**

(a)

| Alpha Ltd |
| --- |
| 121 Baker St |
| Newcastle, NE1 7DJ |
| |
| **REMITTANCE ADVICE** |

**To:** Maximus Ltd                                        **Date:** 31 Aug 20XX

Please find attached our cheque in payment of the following amounts.

| Invoice number | Credit note number | Amount |
| --- | --- | --- |
| 864 | | 6,386 |
| | 252 | 964 |
| | 258 | 1,218 |
| | **Total amount paid** | **4,204** |

(b)    A remittance note is for our records only                                F

A remittance note is sent to a supplier to advise them of
the amount being paid                                                          T

**46    HOLLY LTD**

(a)

Purchase return 286

(b)

£928.80

(c)

£172.00

(d)

£1,032.00

**47    PAINTS R US**

| | |
| --- | --- |
| Has the correct product been supplied? | Y |
| Has the correct net price been calculated? | Y |
| Has the total invoice price been calculated correctly? | N |
| What would be the VAT amount charged if the invoice was correct? | £32.00 |
| What would be the total amount charged if the invoice was correct? | £192.00 |

**48 EP MANUFACTURERS**

(a)

Cheque for £1,200

(b)

Invoice 488

(c)

£4,850.00

**49 STANNY LTD**

(a)

| | Ringo Rings | |
| --- | --- | --- |
| | 37 Parker Lane | |
| | Stoke SK1 0KE | |
| | | |
| | **REMITTANCE ADVICE** | |
| **To:** Stanny Ltd | | **Date:** 31 Mar 20XX |

Please find attached our cheque in payment of the following amounts.

| Invoice number | Credit note number | Amount |
| --- | --- | --- |
| 694 | | 2,300 |
| 658 | | 3,640 |
| | 198 | 650 |
| | 154 | 1,250 |
| | **Total amount paid** | **4,040** |

(b) A remittance note is for ours and the suppliers records     T

A remittance note is sent by a supplier confirming amounts received from them     F

### 50    TOYWORLD

(a)

| Cheque for £500 |
| --- |

(b)

| Invoice 505 |
| --- |

(c)

| £4,000 |
| --- |

### 51    HENRY HOUSE

(a)

**Henry House**

**22 Nursery Road**

**Keighley, BD22 7BD**

**REMITTANCE ADVICE**

**To:** Abbies Party                                                        **Date:** 31 Aug 20XX

Please find attached our cheque in payment of the following amounts.

| Invoice number | Credit note number | Amount |
| --- | --- | --- |
| 242 | | 220 |
| | 27 | 82 |
| | | |
| | | |
| | | |
| **Total amount paid** | | 138 |

(b)    The remittance advice note will be sent to the supplier to advise them of the amount being paid

**52   GREY GARAGES**

**Remittance advice**

**To:** Mulberry Motors

**From:** Grey Garages

**Payment method:**   BACS          **Date of payment:** 25 July

| Items outstanding | | | Tick if included in payment |
|---|---|---|---|
| Date 20XX | Details | Amount £ | |
| 23-Jun | Invoice 213 | 740 | ✓ |
| 06-Jul | Credit note 14 | 120 | ✓ |
| 13-Jul | Invoice 216 | 620 | ✓ |
| 19-Jul | Invoice 257 | 870 | |
| | Total amount paid | £1,240 | |

**53   ERRICO**

| Supplier | £ | Date by which the payment should be received by the supplier |
|---|---|---|
| Giacomo | 67.51 | 11 June 20XX |
| Gaetani | 39.33 | 9 June 20XX |

# DOCUMENTATION AND RECORDS FOR CUSTOMERS

## 54    ALESSANDRO LTD

(a)

| | Alessandro Ltd | | | | |
|---|---|---|---|---|---|
| | 8 Alan Street | | | | |
| | Glasgow, G1 7DJ | | | | |

**VAT Registration No. 398 2774 01**

Palermo Wholesale                                    **Customer account code:**  AGG42

167 Front St

Stanley

DH8 4TJ

**DELIVERY NOTE NUMBER:  24369**

**Date:** 1 Aug 20XX                                    **Invoice No:** 327

| Quantity | Product code | Total list price £ | Net amount after discount £ | VAT £ | Gross £ |
|---|---|---|---|---|---|
| 40 | SB05 | 2,500 | 2,200 | 440 | 2,640 |

(b)

| Prompt payment discount |
|---|

**55    HLB WHOLESALE**

(a)

<table>
<tr><td colspan="6" align="center">

**Painting Supplies Ltd**

**19 Edmund St**

**Newcastle, NE6 5DJ**

**VAT Registration No. 402 2958 02**
</td></tr>
<tr><td colspan="3">

HLB Wholesale

98 Back St

Consett

DH4 3PD
</td><td colspan="3">

**Customer account code:**  HLB24

**Delivery note number:**  46589

**Date:** 1 Feb 20XX
</td></tr>
<tr><td colspan="6">**Invoice No:** 298</td></tr>
<tr>
<td>Quantity</td>
<td>Product code</td>
<td>Total list price £</td>
<td>Net amount after discount £</td>
<td>VAT £</td>
<td>Gross £</td>
</tr>
<tr>
<td>20</td>
<td>SD19</td>
<td>300</td>
<td>270</td>
<td>54</td>
<td>324</td>
</tr>
</table>

(b)

| Trade discount |
| --- |

## 56    MASHED LTD

(a)

<table>
<tr><td colspan="6" align="center">**Hickory House**<br><br>**22 Nursery Road**<br><br>**Keighley, BD22 7BD**<br><br><br>**VAT Registration No. 476 1397 02**</td></tr>
<tr><td colspan="3">Mashed Ltd<br><br>42 Moorside Court<br><br>Ilkley<br><br>Leeds, LS29 4PR<br><br>**Invoice No:** 47</td><td colspan="3">**Customer account code:** MA87<br><br><br>**Delivery note number:** 472<br><br><br>**Date:** 1 Aug 20XX</td></tr>
<tr><td>*Quantity of pots*</td><td>*Product code*</td><td>*Total list price £*</td><td>*Net amount after discount £*</td><td>*VAT £*</td><td>*Gross £*</td></tr>
<tr><td align="center">20</td><td align="center">P10</td><td align="center">100</td><td align="center">90</td><td align="center">18</td><td align="center">108</td></tr>
</table>

(b)

| Bulk discount |
| --- |

## 57    WILLIAM & SAMMY LTD

(a)

| Sales invoice 286 |
| --- |

(b)

| £4,481.28 |
| --- |

(c)

| £4,668.00 |
| --- |

**58    DIAMONDS & RUBIES LTD**

**Stavros**

**121 Baker St**

**Newcastle, NE1 7DJ**

**To:** Diamonds & Rubies Ltd                                      **Date:** 31 Aug 20XX

| Date 20XX | Details | Transaction amount £ | Outstanding amount £ |
|---|---|---|---|
| 5 Aug | Invoice 3927 | 4,640 | 4,640 |
| 10 Aug | Credit note 96 | 980 | 3,660 |
| 21 Aug | Invoice 3964 | 1,560 | 5,220 |
| 28 Aug | Credit note 104 | 650 | 4,570 |
| 30 Aug | Cheque received | 2,100 | 2,470 |

**59    MAX LTD**

**Painting Supplies Ltd**

**19 Edmund St**

**Newcastle, NE6 5DJ**

**To:** Max Ltd                                      **Date:** 28 Feb 20XX

| Date 20XX | Details | Transaction amount £ | Outstanding amount £ |
|---|---|---|---|
| 5 Feb | Invoice 4658 | 2,560 | 2,560 |
| 11 Feb | Invoice 3964 | 3,290 | 5,850 |
| 21 Feb | Credit note 125 | 230 | 5,620 |
| 23 Feb | Credit note 139 | 560 | 5,060 |
| 27 Feb | Cheque received | 1,900 | 3,160 |

## 60   BETA BOARDS

<table>
<tr><td colspan="4" align="center">**Beta Boards**<br>**3 Victoria Avenue**<br>**Troon**<br>**KA5 2BD**</td></tr>
<tr><td colspan="2">**To:** Ava Ltd</td><td colspan="2" align="right">**Date:** 31 Aug 20XX</td></tr>
<tr><td>*Date*<br>*20XX*</td><td>*Details*</td><td align="center">*Transaction amount*<br>£</td><td align="center">*Outstanding amount*<br>£</td></tr>
<tr><td>10 Aug</td><td>Invoice 222</td><td align="center">350</td><td align="center">350</td></tr>
<tr><td>12 Aug</td><td>Cheque</td><td align="center">225</td><td align="center">125</td></tr>
<tr><td>15 Aug</td><td>Invoice 305</td><td align="center">744</td><td align="center">869</td></tr>
<tr><td>20 Aug</td><td>Credit note 194</td><td align="center">339</td><td align="center">530</td></tr>
<tr><td>24 Aug</td><td>Cheque</td><td align="center">530</td><td align="center">0</td></tr>
</table>

# UNDERSTANDING THE DOUBLE ENTRY SYSTEM

## 61   ACCOUNTING EQUATION

(a)   Assets less capital is equal to liabilities                          True

Assets plus liabilities are equal to capital                       False

Capital plus liabilities are equal to assets                      True

(b)

| Item | Asset or liability? |
|------|---------------------|
| Inventory | Asset |
| Machinery | Asset |
| 5 year loan | Liability |

## 62 CLASSIFICATION

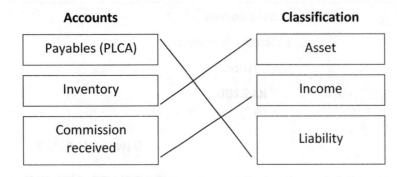

| Accounts | Classification |
|----------|----------------|
| Payables (PLCA) | Asset |
| Inventory | Income |
| Commission received | Liability |

## 63 FINANCIAL ACCOUNTING

(a)

| | |
|---|---|
| Capital is equal to assets plus liabilities | False |
| Assets less liabilities are equal to capital | True |
| Liabilities are equal to capital plus assets | False |

(b)

| Item | Asset or liability? |
|------|---------------------|
| VAT owed to tax authorities | Liability |
| Amounts owing to payables | Liability |
| Money in the bank | Asset |

## 64 CAPEX

| Item | Capital income | Revenue income | Capital expenditure | Revenue expenditure |
|------|----------------|----------------|---------------------|---------------------|
| Receipt from sale of motor vehicle | X | | | |
| Receipts from credit sales | | X | | |
| Purchase of machinery | | | X | |
| Payment of electricity bill | | | | X |
| Purchase of goods for resale | | | | X |

## 65 REVEX

| Item | Capital income | Revenue income | Capital expenditure | Revenue expenditure |
|------|----------------|----------------|---------------------|---------------------|
| Receipt from sale of machinery | X | | | |
| Payment of telephone bill | | | | X |
| Purchase of building | | | X | |
| Receipts from cash sales | | X | | |
| Receipts from credit receivables | | X | | |

## 66   EXPENDITURE TYPES

| Item | Capital expenditure | Revenue expenditure | Capital income | Revenue income |
|---|---|---|---|---|
| Purchase of a new computer system | X | | | |
| Receipts from customers | | | | X |
| Receipt from sale of fixtures and fittings | | | X | |
| Payment of salaries to staff | | X | | |
| Purchase of cleaning materials | | X | | |
| Receipt of bank interest | | | | X |

## 67   ASSET OR LIABILITY

(a)

| Item | Asset or liability? |
|---|---|
| Factory building | Asset |
| Money due to suppliers | Liability |
| Car used in business | Asset |

(b)   **Complete the sentence below by selecting the correct option to show how this transaction will affect the accounts of ABC Co.**

The expense electricity will *increase*, the asset of bank will *decrease*.

## 68   ACCOUNTING EQUATION 2

| Assets | Liabilities | Capital |
|---|---|---|
| £ | £ | £ |
| 158,360 | 28,870 | 129,490 |

# Section 3

# MOCK ASSESSMENT QUESTIONS

**TASK 1.1 (12 marks)**

On 1 December Rocky Ricardo delivered the following goods to a credit customer, Alpha Group.

---

**Rocky Ricardo**

**1 Rocky Way**

**Middleton, M42 5TU**

Delivery note No. 2132

01 Dec 20XX

Alpha Group                                                         **Customer account code:** ALP01

Alpha House

Warwick

WR11 5TB

200 cases of product A, product code A1.

---

The list price of the goods was £10 per case plus VAT. Alpha Group are to be given a 10% trade discount and a 2% prompt payment discount.

(a)     **Complete the invoice below. (4 marks)**

| | | | | | |
|---|---|---|---|---|---|
| **Rocky Ricardo** | | | | | |
| **1 Rocky Way** | | | | | |
| **Middleton, M42 5TU** | | | | | |

VAT Registration No. 298 3827 04

Alpha Group                                   **Customer account code:**
Alpha House
Warwick                                       **Delivery note number:**
WR11 5TB
                                              **Date:** 1 Dec 20XX
**Invoice No:** 950

| Quantity of cases | Product code | Total list price £ | Net amount after discount £ | VAT £ | Gross £ |
|---|---|---|---|---|---|
|  |  |  |  |  |  |

(b)     **What will be the amounts entered into the sales day book after the invoice in (a) has been prepared? (3 marks)**

| Sales day book | | | | | |
|---|---|---|---|---|---|
| **Date 20XX** | **Details** | **Invoice No:** | **Total £** | **VAT £** | **Net £** |
| 1 Dec | Alpha Group | 950 |  |  |  |

(c)     A cheque for £1,000 has now been received from Alpha Group which incorrectly states is full settlement of their account. Their account in the sales ledger is shown below:

**Alpha Group**

| Date 20XX | Details | Amount £ | Date 20XX | Details | Amount £ |
|---|---|---|---|---|---|
| 3 Oct | Bank | 4,288 | 1 Oct | Balance b/f | 4,288 |
| 25 Nov | Purchase returns credit note 102 | 500 | 21 Nov | Purchase invoice 123 | 1,500 |
|  |  |  | 29 Nov | Purchase invoice 189 | 2,000 |

**Which item has not been included in the payment? (2 marks)**

| |
|---|
|  |

Select your account name from the following list: Balance b/f, Purchase invoice 123, Purchase invoice 189, Bank, Purchase returns credit note 102

(d)   An invoice has been sent to Alpha Group for £500 plus VAT of £100. A prompt payment discount of 1% has been offered for payment within 5 days.

(i)   **What is the amount Alpha Group should pay if payment is made within 5 days? (2 marks)**

£

(ii)   **What is the amount Alpha Group should pay if payment is NOT made within 5 days? (1 mark)**

£

## TASK 1.2 (9 marks)

A supply of cardboard boxes has been delivered to Rocky Ricardo's by Echo Ltd. The purchase order sent from Rocky Ricardo's, and the invoice from Echo Ltd, are shown below.

---

**Rocky Ricardo**

**1 Rocky Way**

**Middleton, M42 5TU**

Purchase Order No. RR111

**To:** Echo Ltd

**Date:** 7 Dec 20XX

Please supply 1,000 widgets product code 243

**Purchase price:** £1 per widget, plus VAT

**Discount:** less 10% trade discount, as agreed

---

**Echo Ltd**

**2 Walford Way, Essex, ES4 4XX**

**VAT Registration No. 533 8372 12**

**Invoice No. 123**

Rocky Ricardo

1 Rocky Way

Middleton, M42 5TU

10 Dec 20XX

| 1,000 ........ widgets product code 243  @ £1 each | £1,000.00 |
|---|---|
| VAT | £200.00 |
| Total | £1,200.00 |

**Terms:** 30 days net

---

(a)  **Check the invoice against the purchase order and answer the following questions. (4 marks)**

Has the correct discount been applied?                                          Yes        No

How much should the trade discount amount to?                          £_____

What would be the VAT amount charged if the invoice was correct?   £_____

(b)  The following invoice has been received from the credit supplier Messi Brothers.

| |
|---|
| <div align="center">**Messi Brothers**</div><div align="center">**Unit 3 Fothersway Business Park, Newcastle**</div><div align="center">**VAT Registration No. 933 8982 02**</div><div align="center">**Invoice No. 1365**</div> |

Rocky Ricardo

1 Rocky Way

Middleton, M42 5TU

10 Dec 20XX

| | |
|---|---|
| 500  ........ of product code 1872  @ £3.75 each | £1,875.00 |
| VAT | £375.00 |
| Total | £2,250.00 |

**Terms:** 30 days net

**What will be the details and amounts entered into the day book? (5 marks)**

| Day book: | | | | | |
|---|---|---|---|---|---|
| Date 20XX | Details | Invoice No: | Total £ | VAT £ | Net £ |
| **10 Dec** | | 1365 | | | |

## TASK 1.3 (9 marks)

The two invoices below were received on 20 October from credit suppliers of Lewin & Co who offer prompt payment discounts.

**Invoices:**

| Bridge Brothers | |
|---|---|
| VAT registration 446 4752 01 | |
| Invoice number 193 | |
| To: Lewin & Co 19 October 20XX | |
| | £ |
| 5 product code 895 @ £18.75 each | 93.75 |
| VAT @ 20% | 18.75 |
| | _____ |
| Total | 112.50 |
| Terms: 2% prompt payment discount if payment is received within 4 days of the invoice date. | |

| Mitchells | |
|---|---|
| VAT registration 446 4742 01 | |
| Invoice number 578 | |
| To: Lewin & Co 19 October 20XX | |
| | £ |
| 9 product code 756 @ £13.25 each | 119.25 |
| VAT @ 20% | 23.85 |
| | _____ |
| Total | 143.10 |
| Terms: 10% prompt payment discount if payment is received within 5 days of the invoice date. | |

(a) **Calculate the amount to be paid to each supplier if the prompt payment discount is taken and show the date by which the supplier should receive the payment. (4 marks)**

| Supplier | £ | Date by which the payment should be received by the supplier |
|---|---|---|
| Bridge Brothers | | |
| Mitchells | | |

It is the policy of Lewin & Co to check each supplier statement as they arrive to ensure that they agree to the individual accounts within the purchases ledger. Provided below is the statement of account from Xcess Stock and their account in the purchases ledger.

Lewin & Co's policy is to only pay for items from the supplier statement which appear in their account in the purchases ledger.

(b) **Place a tick next to the 3 items in the supplier statement which will not be included within the payment. (3 marks)**

| Date 20XX | Details | Amount £ | Date 20XX | Details | Amount £ |
|---|---|---|---|---|---|
| 21 Dec | Credit note 101 | 940 | 12 Dec | Invoice 1001 | 1,700 |
| | | | 21 Dec | Invoice 1004 | 2,350 |
| 31 Dec | Balance c/d | 3,580 | 27 Dec | Invoice 1010 | 470 |
| | | **4,520** | | | **4,520** |
| | | | 20XY 1 Jan | Balance b/d | 3,580 |

| | | |
|---|---|---|
| **Xcess Stock** <br> **Unit 7 Windy Industrial Estate** <br> **Irvine, KA6 8HU** <br> **To:** Lewin & Co <br> **Date:** 31 Dec 20XX | | Not to be paid |

| Date 20XX | Details | Transaction amount £ | |
|---|---|---|---|
| 12 Dec | Invoice 1001 | 1,700 | |
| 13 Dec | Invoice 1003 | 1,500 | |
| 21 Dec | Invoice 1004 | 2,350 | |
| 21 Dec | Credit note 101 | 940 | |
| 22 Dec | Invoice 1005 | 450 | |
| 27 Dec | Invoice 1010 | 470 | |
| 28 Dec | Credit note 102 | 50 | |

(c)   **What will be the amount paid to Xcess Stock by Lewin & Co? (1 mark)**

| |
|---|
| |

(d)   One of the accounts within the purchases ledger of Lewin & Co is for the credit supplier Minto Madness. A credit note for a prompt payment discount of £20 plus VAT has been received from Minto Madness. Before processing the credit note, the balance on the account of Minto Madness is £1,540.

**What is the amount remaining on the account taking into consideration the credit note? (1 mark)**

| |
|---|
| |

### TASK 1.4 (15 marks)

There are five payments to be entered in Carter's cash-book.

**Receipts**

| Received cash with thanks for goods bought. | Received cash with thanks for goods bought. |
|---|---|
| From Carter's, a customer without a credit account. | From Carter's, a customer without a credit account. |
| Net £800 | Net £200 |
| VAT £160 | VAT £40 |
| Total £960 | Total £240 |
| *J Pumpkin* | *B Row* |

**Cheque book counterfoils**

| Lemon Ltd | Remo Motor | Fencer |
|---|---|---|
| (Purchase ledger account LEM002) | (no credit account) | (Purchase ledger account FEN001) |
| | £240 including VAT | |
| £100 | | £600 |
| 000123 | 000124 | 000125 |

(a) **Enter the details from the two receipts and three cheque book stubs into the credit side of the cash-book shown below and total each column. (6 marks)**

**Cash book – credit side**

| Details | Cash | Bank | VAT | Payables | Cash purchases | Motor expenses |
|---|---|---|---|---|---|---|
| Balance b/f | | 11,450 | | | | |
| J Pumpkin | | | | | | |
| B Row | | | | | | |
| Lemon Ltd | | | | | | |
| Remo Motor | | | | | | |
| Fencer | | | | | | |
| **Total** | | | | | | |

There are two cheques from credit customers to be entered in Carter's cash book:

Jeff Jolly     £127

Dolly Darton     £310

(b) **Enter the above details into the debit side of the cash-book and total each column. (4 marks)**

**Cash book – debit side**

| Details | Cash | Bank | Receivables |
|---|---|---|---|
| Balance b/f | 1,850 | | |
| Jeff Jolly | | | |
| Dolly Darton | | | |
| Total | | | |

(c) **Using your answers to (a) and (b) above, calculate the cash balance. (2 marks)**

£

(d) **Using your answers to (a) and (b) above, calculate the bank balance. (2 marks)**

£

(e) **Will the bank balance calculated in (d) above be a debit or credit balance? (1 mark)**

Debit/Credit

## TASK 1.5 (15 marks)

The business maintains a petty cash book as both a book of prime entry and part of the double entry accounting system. The petty cash book has been partly completed for the month of June. The following transactions all took place on 30 June.

Office Supplies paid £72 including VAT

Postage paid £10 no VAT

(a) **Enter the above transactions, in the order in which they are shown, in the petty cash-book below. (8 marks)**

(b) **Total the petty cash-book and show the balance carried down as at 30th June. (6 marks)**

Select your entries for the 'Details' columns from the following list: Amount, Balance b/d, Balance c/d, Details, Office Supplies, Postage, VAT, Motor expenses

**Petty cash-book**

| Date 20XX | Details | Amount £ | Date 20XX | Details | Amount £ | VAT £ | Postage £ | Motor expenses £ | Office supplies £ |
|---|---|---|---|---|---|---|---|---|---|
| 23 Jun | Balance b/f | 100.00 | 30 Jun | Fuel | 38.40 | 6.40 | | 32.00 | |
| 23 Jun | Bank | 100.00 | 30 Jun | Office supplies | 24.00 | 4.00 | | | 20.00 |
| | | | | | | | | | |
| | | | | | | | | | |

(c) **What is the amount required to restore to the imprest level of £200? (1 mark)**

**TASK 1.6 (12 marks)**

The following transactions all took place on 31 July and have been entered into the discounts allowed day book of Roland's as shown below. No entries have yet been made into the ledger system.

| Date 20XX | Details | Credit note number | Total £ | VAT £ | Net £ |
|---|---|---|---|---|---|
| 31 July | Aldo & Co | 45 | 24.00 | 4.00 | 20.00 |
| 31 July | Hopley Brothers | 46 | 36.00 | 6.00 | 30.00 |
| 31 July | Fernando's | 47 | 25.20 | 4.20 | 21.00 |
| 31 July | Richmond Travel | 48 | 38.40 | 6.40 | 32.00 |
| | **Totals** | | 123.60 | 20.60 | 103.00 |

(a)     **What will be the entries in the general ledger? (6 marks)**

| Account name | Amount £ | Debit ✓ | Credit ✓ |
|---|---|---|---|
| | | | |
| | | | |
| | | | |

(b)     **What will be the entries in the subsidiary ledger? (6 marks)**

| Account name | Amount £ | Debit ✓ | Credit ✓ |
|---|---|---|---|
| | | | |
| | | | |
| | | | |
| | | | |

## TASK 1.7 (12 marks)

Roger's cash book is both a book of prime entry and part of the double entry bookkeeping system. The following transactions all took place on 31 December and have been entered in the debit side of the cash-book as shown below.

**Cash-book – Debit side**

| Date 20XX | Details | Cash £ | Bank £ |
|---|---|---|---|
| 31 Dec | Balance b/f | 200 | 2,883 |
| 31 Dec | TUV Ltd | | 4,000 |

(a) **What will be the entry in the sales ledger? (3 marks)**

**Sales ledger**

| Account name | Amount £ | Debit ✓ | Credit ✓ |
|---|---|---|---|
| | | | |

(b) **What will be the entry in the general ledger? (3 marks)**

**General ledger**

| Account name | Amount £ | Debit ✓ | Credit ✓ |
|---|---|---|---|
| | | | |

The following transactions all took place on 31 December and have been entered in the credit side of the cash-book as shown below. No entries have yet been made in the ledgers.

**Cash-book – Credit side**

| Date 20XX | Details | VAT £ | Cash £ | Bank £ |
|---|---|---|---|---|
| 31 Dec | Entertainment | 32 | | 192 |
| 31 Dec | Insurance | | | 240 |

(c) **What will be the entries in the general ledger? (6 marks)**

**General ledger**

| Account name | Amount £ | Debit ✓ | Credit ✓ |
|---|---|---|---|
| | | | |
| | | | |
| | | | |

**TASK 1.8 (12 marks)**

The following is a summary of transactions up to 31 December 20XX for Bella Pumpkin, a new credit customer.

| |
|---|
| £1,700 re invoice 1001 of 12 Dec |
| £2,350 re invoice 1004 of 21 Dec |
| £940 re credit note 101 of 21 Dec |
| £470 re invoice 1010 of 27 Dec |
| Cheque for £2,000 received 29 Dec |

(a)  **Enter the transactions into the sales ledger of Bella Pumpkin. (5 marks)**

(b)  **Insert the balance carried down and the balance brought down together with date and details. (2 marks)**

**Bella Pumpkin**

| Date 20XX | Details | Amount £ | Date 20XX | Details | Amount £ |
|---|---|---|---|---|---|
| | | | | | |
| | | | | | |
| | | | | | |
| | | | | | |
| | | | | | |

(c)  **Complete the statement of account below to be sent to Bella Pumpkin (5 marks)**

**Rocky Ricardo**

**1 Rocky Way**

**Middleton, M42 5TU**

**To:** Bella Pumpkin                                            **Date:** 31 Dec 20XX

| Date 20XX | Details | Transaction amount £ | Outstanding amount £ |
|---|---|---|---|
| | | | |
| | | | |
| | | | |
| | | | |
| | | | |

## TASK 1.9 (12 marks)

Below is a list of balances to be transferred to the trial balance as at 31 December.

**Place the figures in the debit or credit column, as appropriate, and total each column.**

| Account name | Amount £ | Debit £ | Credit £ |
|---|---|---|---|
| Motor vehicles | 27,268 | | |
| Inventory | 18,592 | | |
| Bank overdraft | 12,333 | | |
| Petty cash control | 200 | | |
| Sales ledger control (SLCA) | 169,037 | | |
| Purchases ledger control (PLCA) | 46,086 | | |
| VAT owing to tax authorities (HMRC) | 53,376 | | |
| Capital | 19,364 | | |
| Loan from bank | 16,413 | | |
| Sales | 550,064 | | |
| Sales returns | 38,873 | | |
| Purchases | 263,387 | | |
| Purchases returns | 674 | | |
| Discount received | 1,800 | | |
| Discount allowed | 2,440 | | |
| Wages | 152,199 | | |
| Motor expenses | 2,953 | | |
| Stationery | 2,450 | | |
| Rent and rates | 10,345 | | |
| Advertising | 1,262 | | |
| Hotel expenses | 1,224 | | |
| Telephone | 1,599 | | |
| Subscriptions | 262 | | |
| Miscellaneous expenses | 8,019 | | |
| **Totals** | | | |

**TASK 1.10 (12 marks)**

(a)  It is important to understand the difference between capital expenditure, revenue expenditure, capital income and revenue income.

**Select one option in each instance below to show whether the item will be capital expenditure, revenue expenditure, capital income or revenue income. (6 marks)**

| Item | Capital expenditure | Revenue expenditure | Capital income | Revenue income |
|---|---|---|---|---|
| Purchase of computer equipment | | | | |
| Receipts from credit sales | | | | |
| Receipt from sale of motor vehicle (non current asset) | | | | |
| Purchase of motor vehicle | | | | |
| Purchase of stationery | | | | |
| Payment of rent | | | | |

(b)  **Show whether the following statements are true or false. (3 marks)**

| | | |
|---|---|---|
| Assets less liabilities are equal to capital | True | False |
| The business and owner are two separate entities | True | False |
| A debit increases an item of income | True | False |

(c)  **Classify each of the following items as an asset or a liability. (3 marks)**

| Item | Asset or liability? |
|---|---|
| Computer equipment | Select<br><br>Asset OR Liability |
| Petty cash | Select<br><br>Asset OR Liability |
| Money owed to suppliers | Select<br><br>Asset OR Liability |

# Section 4

# MOCK ASSESSMENT ANSWERS

**TASK 1.1 (12 marks)**

(a)

| | | | | | |
|---|---|---|---|---|---|
| | | **Rocky Ricardo** | | | |
| | | **1 Rocky Way** | | | |
| | | **Middleton, M42 5TU** | | | |
| | | VAT Registration No. 298 3827 04 | | | |

Alpha Group **Customer account code:** ALP01

Alpha House

Warwick **Delivery note number:** 2132

WR11 5TB

**Date:** 1 Dec 20XX

**Invoice No:** 950

| Quantity of cases | Product code | Total list price £ | Net amount after discount £ | VAT £ | Gross £ |
|---|---|---|---|---|---|
| 200 | A1 | 2,000 | 1,800 | 360 | 2,160 |

(b)

| Sales day book | | | | | |
|---|---|---|---|---|---|
| **Date 20XX** | **Details** | **Invoice No:** | **Total £** | **VAT £** | **Net £** |
| 1 Dec | Alpha Group | 950 | 2,160 | 360 | 1,800 |

(c)     Purchase invoice 189

(d)     (i)

| £594 |
|------|

        (ii)

| £600 |
|------|

## TASK 1.2 (9 marks)

(a)     Has the correct discount been applied?                                                    No

        How much should the trade discount amount to?                                   £100

        What would be the VAT amount charged if the invoice was correct?        £180

(b)

| Day book: Purchases day book | | | | | |
|---|---|---|---|---|---|
| Date 20XX | Details | Invoice No: | Total £ | VAT £ | Net £ |
| 10 Dec | Messi Brothers | 1365 | 2,250 | 375 | 1,875 |

## TASK 1.3 (9 marks)

(a)

| Supplier | £ | Date by which the payment should be received by the supplier |
|---|---|---|
| Bridge Brothers | 110.25 | 23rd October |
| Mitchells | 128.79 | 24th October |

(b)

| Xcess Stock<br>Unit 7 Windy Industrial Estate<br>Irvine, KA6 8HU<br>**To:** Lewin & Co<br>**Date:** 31 Dec 20XX | | | Not to<br>be paid |
|---|---|---|---|
| Date<br>20XX | Details | Transaction<br>amount<br>£ | |
| 12 Dec | Invoice 1001 | 1,700 | |
| 13 Dec | Invoice 1003 | 1,500 | ✓ |
| 21 Dec | Invoice 1004 | 2,350 | |
| 21 Dec | Credit note 101 | 940 | |
| 22 Dec | Invoice 1005 | 450 | ✓ |
| 27 Dec | Invoice 1010 | 470 | |
| 28 Dec | Credit note 102 | 50 | ✓ |

(c)    £3,580

(d)    £1,516

## TASK 1.4 (15 marks)

(a)    **Cash book – credit side**

| Details | Cash | Bank | VAT | Payables | Cash<br>purchases | Motor<br>expenses |
|---|---|---|---|---|---|---|
| Balance b/f | | 11,450 | | | | |
| J Pumpkin | 960 | | 160 | | 800 | |
| B Row | 240 | | 40 | | 200 | |
| Lemon Ltd | | 100 | | 100 | | |
| Remo Motor | | 240 | 40 | | | 200 |
| Fencer | | 600 | | 600 | | |
| Total | 1,200 | 12,390 | 240 | 700 | 1,000 | 200 |

(b)    **Cash book – debit side**

| Details | Cash | Bank | Receivables |
|---|---|---|---|
| Balance b/f | 1,850 | | |
| Jeff Jolly | | 127 | 127 |
| Dolly Darton | | 310 | 310 |
| Total | 1,850 | 437 | 437 |

(c)    £650

(d)    £11,953

(e)    Credit

## TASK 1.5 (15 marks)

(a) – (b)

**Petty cash-book**

| Date 20XX | Details | Amount £ | Date 20XX | Details | Amount £ | VAT £ | Postage £ | Motor expenses £ | Office supplies £ |
|---|---|---|---|---|---|---|---|---|---|
| 23 Jun | Balance b/f | 100.00 | 30 Jun | Fuel | 38.40 | 6.40 | | 32.00 | |
| 23 Jun | Bank | 100.00 | 30 Jun | Office supplies | 24.00 | 4.00 | | | 20.00 |
| | | | 30 Jun | Office supplies | 72.00 | 12.00 | | | 60.00 |
| | | | 30 Jun | Postage | 10.00 | | 10.00 | | |
| | | | 30 Jun | Bal c/d | 55.60 | | | | |
| | | 200.00 | | | 200.00 | 22.40 | 10.00 | 32.00 | 80.00 |

(c)    £144.40

## TASK 1.6 (12 marks)

(a)    **What will be the entries in the general ledger?**

| Account name | Amount £ | Debit ✓ | Credit ✓ |
|---|---|---|---|
| Sales ledger control | 123.60 | | ✓ |
| VAT | 20.60 | ✓ | |
| Discounts allowed | 103.00 | ✓ | |

**(b)** **What will be the entries in the subsidiary ledger?**

| Account name | Amount £ | Debit ✓ | Credit ✓ |
|---|---|---|---|
| Aldo & Co | 24.00 | | ✓ |
| Hopley Brothers | 36.00 | | ✓ |
| Fernando's | 25.20 | | ✓ |
| Richmond Travel | 38.40 | | ✓ |

## TASK 1.7 (12 marks)

**(a)** **Sales ledger**

| Account name | Amount £ | Debit ✓ | Credit ✓ |
|---|---|---|---|
| TUV Ltd | 4,000 | | ✓ |

**(b)** **General ledger**

| Account name | Amount £ | Debit ✓ | Credit ✓ |
|---|---|---|---|
| Sales ledger control | 4,000 | | ✓ |

**(c)** **General ledger**

| Account name | Amount £ | Debit ✓ | Credit ✓ |
|---|---|---|---|
| Entertainment | 160 | ✓ | |
| VAT | 32 | ✓ | |
| Insurance | 240 | ✓ | |

**TASK 1.8 (12 marks)**

(a) – (d)

### Bella Pumpkin

| Date 20XX | Details | Amount £ | Date 20XX | Details | Amount £ |
|---|---|---|---|---|---|
| 12 Dec | Invoice 1001 | 1,700 | 21 Dec | Credit note 101 | 940 |
| 21 Dec | Invoice 1004 | 2,350 | 29 Dec | Cheque rec'd | 2,000 |
| 27 Dec | Invoice 1010 | 470 | 31 Dec | Balance c/d | 1,580 |
| | | **4,520** | | | **4,520** |
| 20XY 1 Jan | Balance b/d | 1,580 | | | |

(e)

### Rocky Ricardo
### 1 Rocky Way
### Middleton, M42 5TU

**To:** Bella Pumpkin                          **Date:** 31 Dec 20XX

| Date 20XX | Details | Transaction amount £ | Outstanding amount £ |
|---|---|---|---|
| 12 Dec | Invoice 1001 | 1,700 | 1,700 |
| 21 Dec | Invoice 1004 | 2,350 | 4,050 |
| 21 Dec | Credit note 101 | 940 | 3,110 |
| 27 Dec | Invoice 1010 | 470 | 3,580 |
| 29 Dec | Cheque | 2,000 | 1,580 |

**TASK 1.9 (12 marks)**

| Account name | Amount £ | Debt £ | Credit £ |
|---|---|---|---|
| Motor vehicles | 27,268 | 27,268 | |
| Inventory | 18,592 | 18,592 | |
| Bank overdraft | 12,333 | | 12,333 |
| Petty cash control | 200 | 200 | |
| Sales ledger control (SLCA) | 169,037 | 169,037 | |
| Purchases ledger control (PLCA) | 46,086 | | 46,086 |
| VAT owing to tax authorities (HMRC) | 53,376 | | 53,376 |
| Capital | 19,364 | | 19,364 |
| Loan from bank | 16,413 | | 16,413 |
| Sales | 550,064 | | 550,064 |
| Sales returns | 38,873 | 38,873 | |
| Purchases | 263,387 | 263,387 | |
| Purchases returns | 674 | | 674 |
| Discount received | 1,800 | | 1,800 |
| Discount allowed | 2,440 | 2,440 | |
| Wages | 152,199 | 152,199 | |
| Motor expenses | 2,953 | 2,953 | |
| Stationery | 2,450 | 2,450 | |
| Rent and rates | 10,345 | 10,345 | |
| Advertising | 1,262 | 1,262 | |
| Hotel expenses | 1,224 | 1,224 | |
| Telephone | 1,599 | 1,599 | |
| Subscriptions | 262 | 262 | |
| Miscellaneous expenses | 8,019 | 8,019 | |
| **Totals** | | 700,110 | 700,110 |

**TASK 1.10 (12 marks)**

(a)

| Item | Capital expenditure | Revenue expenditure | Capital income | Revenue income |
|---|---|---|---|---|
| Purchase of computer equipment | ✓ | | | |
| Receipts from credit sales | | | | ✓ |
| Receipt from sale of motor vehicle (non current asset) | | | ✓ | |
| Purchase of motor vehicle | ✓ | | | |
| Purchase of stationery | | ✓ | | |
| Payment of rent | | ✓ | | |

(b)

| | |
|---|---|
| Assets less liabilities are equal to capital | **True** |
| The business and owner are two separate entities | **True** |
| A debit increases an item of income | **False** |

(c)

| Item | Asset or liability? |
|---|---|
| Computer equipment | Asset |
| Petty cash | Asset |
| Money owed to suppliers | Liability |